Key Stage Three

Geography

Complete Study and Practice

Contents

Contents

Published by CGP

Editors:
David Maliphant and Heather McClelland.

Contributors:
Rosalind Browning, Margaret Collinson, Leigh Edwards, Paddy Gannon, Catherine Hitchcock,
Barbara Melbourne, Mark Ollis, Rebecca Rider, Susan Ross, Dennis Watts.

With thanks to Joe Brazier, Charlotte Burrows and Glenn Rogers for the proofreading.

ISBN: 978 1 84146 392 6

With thanks to Jan Greenway for the copyright research.

*Graph on page 37 showing climate change in Greenland over the last 20,000 years reproduced with thanks to the
NOAA for the graphic and to the Alley (2000) paper for the underlying data.*

*Graph of the last 1000 years of climate change on page 37 adapted from IPCC, 2013: In: Climate Change 2013: The
Physical Science Basis. Contribution of Working Group I to the Fifth Assessment Report of the Intergovernmental Panel
on Climate Change, Box TS.5, Figure 1(b) [Stocker, T.F., D. Qin, G.-K. Plattner, M. Tignor, S.K. Allen, J. Boschung, A.
Nauels, Y. Xia, V. Bex and P.M. Midgley (eds.)]. Cambridge University Press, Cambridge, United Kingdom and New
York, NY, USA.*

World Urban Population Graph on page 81 reproduced with kind permission from Jean-Paul Rodrigue.

With thanks to iStockphoto.com for permission to reproduce the photograph used on page 84.

*Pie chart for UK employment in 2014 on page 104 adapted from data from the Office for National Statistics
licensed under the Open Government Licence v.3.0. http://www.nationalarchives.gov.uk/doc/open-government-
licence/version/3/*

*Vegetation graphic on page 128 adapted from data courtesy of University of Texas Libraries,
The University of Texas at Austin. Original source data 'Central intelligence Agency'.*

Landsat imagery on pages 131 and 135 courtesy of USGS/NASA Landsat.

Population pyramids on page 136 based on data from The World Factbook *2013-14. Washington, DC: Central
Intelligence Agency, 2013.*

*Data used to construct the pie charts on page 136 from the World Bank. Dataset name: Jobs.
Data source: International Labour Organization, Key Indicators of the Labour Market database.*

*Data used to construct the climate graphs for Lagos and Osaka on page 137 from the
U.S. National Climatic Data Center.*

*This product includes mapping data licensed from Ordnance Survey® © Crown copyright 2014.
Ordnance Survey Licence No. 100034841*

www.cgpbooks.co.uk
Printed by Elanders Ltd, Newcastle upon Tyne.
Clipart from Corel®

Based on the classic CGP style created by Richard Parsons.

Our World

Geography is all about the <u>world</u> you <u>live</u> in. This section will help you find out more about some <u>important places</u> and the <u>people</u> that live there.

The **World** is divided into **Continents**

1) <u>Continents</u> are large masses of land and the islands closest to them.

2) Most countries are entirely part of <u>one</u> continent, but some countries span <u>two</u> continents.

3) There are <u>seven continents</u> in the world. Make sure you know them all:

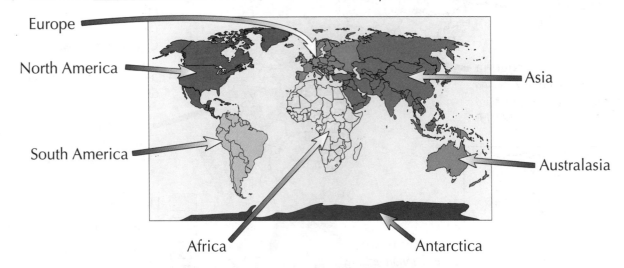

Europe
North America
Asia
South America
Australasia
Africa
Antarctica

The world can also be divided into **Biomes**

1) A <u>biome</u> is an area with distinctive <u>climate</u> and <u>vegetation</u>, e.g. a tropical rainforest or a desert.

2) Biomes usually cover a <u>large area</u>, often spanning <u>multiple countries</u>.

3) The map below shows the world split into <u>ten biomes</u>.

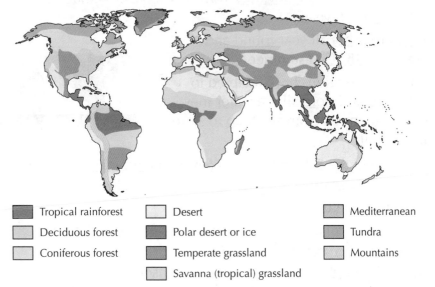

- Tropical rainforest
- Deciduous forest
- Coniferous forest
- Desert
- Polar desert or ice
- Temperate grassland
- Savanna (tropical) grassland
- Mediterranean
- Tundra
- Mountains

Learn the names of the continents wand all the biomes

They may almost all start with 'A', but you really don't want to get your continents muddled up. Make sure you can <u>label</u> them all on a <u>world map</u>. Remember that a continent can have many <u>different biomes</u> — you'll find out more about this later in the section.

Africa

Africa covers <u>20%</u> of Earth's <u>land surface</u> and is the <u>least wealthy</u> continent.

Africa is a Continent made up of Over 50 Countries

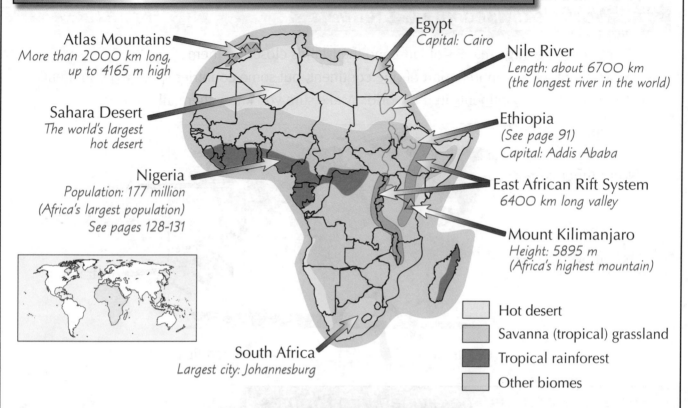

Atlas Mountains
More than 2000 km long, up to 4165 m high

Sahara Desert
The world's largest hot desert

Nigeria
Population: 177 million (Africa's largest population) See pages 128-131

South Africa
Largest city: Johannesburg

Egypt
Capital: Cairo

Nile River
Length: about 6700 km (the longest river in the world)

Ethiopia
(See page 91) Capital: Addis Ababa

East African Rift System
6400 km long valley

Mount Kilimanjaro
Height: 5895 m (Africa's highest mountain)

Hot desert

Savanna (tropical) grassland

Tropical rainforest

Other biomes

There are Several Different Biomes in Africa

Africa contains areas of <u>hot desert</u>, <u>savanna grassland</u> and <u>tropical rainforest</u>.

1) Africa contains the largest hot desert in the world — the <u>Sahara Desert</u>.

   - Deserts <u>lack water</u> and <u>rainfall varies</u> from year to year — much of the Sahara receives <u>less</u> than <u>20 mm</u> each year.

   - The <u>temperature</u> is <u>hot</u> all year round and can average over <u>38 °C</u> in summer.

   - Plants in hot desert regions have adapted to <u>conserve</u>, <u>absorb</u> and <u>store</u> all the <u>water</u> they can, e.g. cacti have <u>stems</u> that can <u>swell up</u> to store water after rainfall.

   cacti

   Thorn bushes have tiny leaves to reduce water loss

   Long roots to reach water supplies

2) Most of Africa south of the Sahara Desert is <u>Savanna (Tropical) Grassland</u>.

   - Savanna areas have <u>wet</u> and <u>dry seasons</u> — almost all of the annual rainfall occurs in the <u>wet season</u>.

   - Temperatures are warm all year round, but the <u>wet season</u> (20-30 °C) is <u>warmer</u> than the <u>dry season</u> (10-20 °C).

   - The vegetation is <u>adapted</u> to survive <u>long dry seasons</u>. For example, grasses <u>die down</u> in the dry season and some trees have <u>long roots</u> to reach the water table.

   - Bushes and trees are <u>less common</u> in areas where <u>human activities</u> (like farming) occur.

3) There are also large areas of <u>tropical rainforest</u> in countries like Ivory Coast, Ghana and Madagascar — see page 4 for more on the tropical rainforest biome.

Africa

Over **1 billion** people live in **Africa**

Asia has the largest population — 4.4 billion people

1) Africa has the second largest population of any continent — 1.1 billion people.

2) Countries in Africa generally have a very youthful population.
E.g. in Kenya, 42.1% of the population are under 14 years old.

3) The population in Africa is growing rapidly because the birth rate is high (36 per 1000 people per year) and the death rate is low (11 per 1000 people per year).

4) Many countries in Africa are poor and at a low level of development. E.g. in Ethiopia the average life expectancy is about 61 years (low) and the literacy rate is 39% (very low).

5) A few countries are more wealthy and developed. E.g. in Egypt the average life expectancy is about 74 years and the literacy rate is 74%.

See section 6 for more on population and section 7 for more on development.

Water affects **Population Density**

1) Population density is the number of people in a given area.

2) Large parts of Africa are deserts where water is very scarce. These places have a low population density (people need water to drink, cook with, wash in and to grow crops).

3) Cities have the highest population density.
Many cities in Africa are found:

- In river basins, e.g. Cairo (capital of Egypt) in the Nile river basin.
- Near a lake, e.g. Kampala (capital of Uganda) next to Lake Victoria.
- On the coast, e.g. Algiers (capital of Algeria) on the northern coast of Africa.

Gross National Income varies a lot between countries

> **Gross National Income (GNI) per head is the total value of goods and services people of that nationality produce in a year, divided by the population of the country.**

1) Many countries in Africa have a low GNI per head. E.g. Democratic Republic of the Congo has the lowest GNI per head in Africa — 230 US Dollars. Farming is the main source of food and income for most of the population.

2) A few countries in Africa have a much higher GNI per head.
E.g. Equatorial Guinea has the highest GNI per head in Africa — 13 560 US Dollars. This is mainly because the country exports a lot of oil, but the wealth is shared very unequally among the population.

Remember — Africa is NOT a country, it's a continent

You really would be surprised how many people make that mistake. Africa is made up of loads of countries, so it's a very large and very diverse continent that's home to over 1 billion people. Make sure you learn the human and physical characteristics on these pages.

Asia — India

India is a country in south <u>Asia</u>. It's home to <u>1.2 billion people</u> and covers a large area — more than <u>3.2 million km²</u>.

The *Capital* of *India* is *New Delhi*

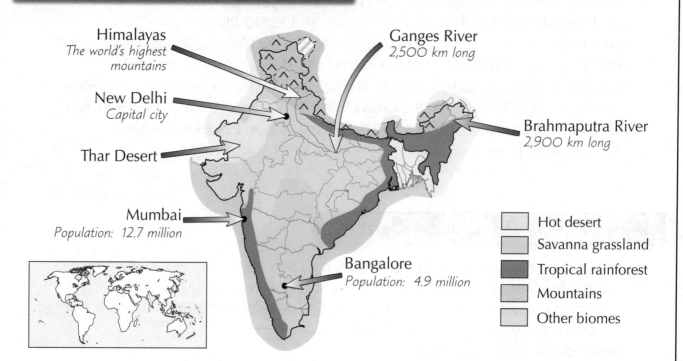

Himalayas
The world's highest mountains

New Delhi
Capital city

Thar Desert

Mumbai
Population: 12.7 million

Ganges River
2,500 km long

Brahmaputra River
2,900 km long

Bangalore
Population: 4.9 million

Hot desert
Savanna grassland
Tropical rainforest
Mountains
Other biomes

India is mostly *Tropical Rainforest*, *Savanna* and *Mountains*

India has large areas of <u>savanna grassland</u> and <u>hot desert</u> (see p.2), as well as <u>mountain biome</u> (see p.6) and <u>tropical rainforest</u>.

1) Most of India has a <u>tropical climate</u>.

2) Some parts (e.g. Bangalore) have a <u>wet</u> and a <u>dry</u> season — good for savanna (tropical) grassland.

3) Other parts of India are hot all year round and receive lots of rain. These conditions are perfect for <u>tropical rainforests</u>.

45m

Canopy layer

Lower tree layer

0

Undergrowth

- A <u>tropical rainforest</u> has hot, humid, growing conditions with many different species — it has <u>two tree layers</u> and a <u>sparse undergrowth layer</u>.

- The <u>canopy layer</u> is full of tall trees like mahogany. Beneath them are <u>smaller trees</u> and climbing plants but there's <u>not much undergrowth</u> due to the <u>lack of light</u>.

- Plants have to be <u>adapted</u> to the heavy rainfall. Most plants have <u>thick, waxy, pointed leaves</u> which water runs off.

- In the past India had a much larger area of tropical rainforest. Now large parts of it have been <u>cleared</u> for logs and grazing.

Asia — India

India has the Second-Largest Population in the World

1) The population of India is huge — <u>over 1.2 billion</u>.

2) India has a <u>young population</u> — 28.5% are under 15 years old.

3) The population is <u>growing steadily</u> because the <u>birth rate</u> is quite <u>high</u> (20 per 1000 people per year) and the <u>death rate</u> is <u>low</u> (7 per 1000 people per year).

4) India is a <u>Newly Industrialised Country</u> (<u>NIC</u>). This means it is getting richer as its economy switches from <u>primary industry</u> (e.g. farming) to <u>secondary</u> and <u>tertiary industry</u> (e.g. manufacturing products and providing services) — see pages 100-101.

5) NICs are <u>more developed</u> than LEDCs, but not as developed as countries like the UK.

   - The average <u>life expectancy</u> is <u>low</u> in India — about 68 years.
   - India's <u>literacy rate</u> is 62.8%

China has the largest population — see p.7

See pages 90-91 for more on these measures of development

Most People in India Don't Live in Cities

1) Only about <u>30% of the population</u> live in <u>urban areas</u> (towns and cities).

2) Most towns and cities are growing rapidly though. There is a <u>high rate</u> of <u>migration into urban areas</u> from the countryside as people seek out better <u>job opportunities</u>.

3) Although most people don't live in cities, India has some of the <u>largest urban areas</u> in the world — like Delhi, Mumbai and Bangalore.

India has a Large Economy but a Low GNI per Head

1) India has a <u>very large economy</u> — the ninth largest in the world.

2) But because India also has a very large population, the <u>GNI per head</u> (average income) is <u>low</u> — just 1550 US Dollars per year.

3) <u>Farming</u> is a major part of the economy. <u>Half</u> the population are dependent on agriculture for their income.

4) The <u>textiles</u> (clothing and fabric) industry is another sector that provides many with a livelihood.

5) India is <u>getting wealthier</u> quite quickly — its GNI is <u>growing</u> by <u>4.6%</u> each year.

6) But wealth is India is <u>unevenly distributed</u>. About <u>30%</u> of the population live in <u>poverty</u>.

7) Many people <u>cannot afford</u> proper <u>housing</u> or <u>sanitation</u> — both in cities and rural areas.

Take a look back at page 3 to remind yourself about GNI per head.

Farmers working in a paddy (rice) field

India — just one country, but full of variety

With over a billion residents, it's not surprising that India is full of contrasts. There are <u>enormous urban areas</u> like Delhi, but at the same time the majority of the population live in small rural villages. You need to know the key facts, and don't skip the vegetation.

Asia — China

There are <u>more people</u> in China than <u>any other country</u> in the world.

Beijing is the **Capital** of China, *Shanghai* is the **Largest City**

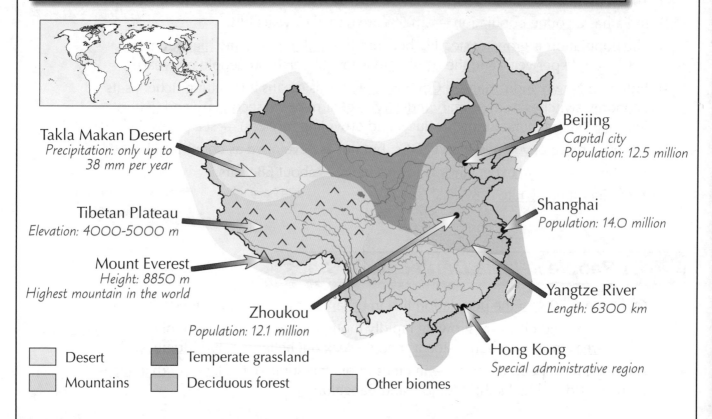

Takla Makan Desert
*Precipitation: only up to
38 mm per year*

Tibetan Plateau
Elevation: 4000-5000 m

Mount Everest
*Height: 8850 m
Highest mountain in the world*

Zhoukou
Population: 12.1 million

Beijing
*Capital city
Population: 12.5 million*

Shanghai
Population: 14.0 million

Yangtze River
Length: 6300 km

Hong Kong
Special administrative region

☐ Desert
☐ Mountains
☐ Temperate grassland
☐ Deciduous forest
☐ Other biomes

There are **Lots** *of* **Different Biomes** *in China*

China has areas of <u>mountains</u>, <u>desert</u>, <u>deciduous forest</u> and <u>temperate grassland</u>.

1) The largest area of <u>mountains</u> in China is the <u>Tibetan Plateau</u>.

- <u>Temperatures</u> in mountains are usually <u>cold</u>, and temperature decreases the higher up you go. <u>Valleys</u> in the plateau can be a lot <u>warmer</u> though — up to 30 °C.

- The plateau doesn't get much <u>precipitation</u> (only <u>460 mm</u> each year), so <u>short grasses</u> that are adapted to cold and dry conditions are the main vegetation.

- <u>Farming</u> on the plateau is <u>difficult</u> and it's not easy to grow crops. Traditionally farmers have been <u>nomads</u> herding <u>livestock</u> over large areas to make the best of the land.

2) Lots of central and northern China is <u>temperate grassland</u>.

- Temperate grasslands have <u>cold winters</u> and <u>hot summers</u>.

- China's temperate grassland areas get lots <u>more rainfall</u> (up to 700 mm each year) than the Tibetan plateau. Most rainfall happens in late <u>spring</u> and early <u>summer</u>.

- Grasses can grow higher than in mountains because its warmer and there's more rain. This means temperate grasslands are good areas for growing <u>cereals</u> like <u>wheat</u>.

3) There are <u>deciduous forests</u> in the east of China (where the climate is less harsh).

- Deciduous forests have <u>milder winters</u> and <u>cooler summers</u> than temperate grasslands.

- Rainfall is <u>highest</u> in China's deciduous forests — they receive up to <u>1500 mm</u> of precipitation each year.

Asia — China

China has the **World's Largest Population**

1) China is the <u>largest country in the world</u> by population — over <u>1.3 billion people live there</u>.
2) China's population is <u>growing</u> because the birth rate (12 per 1000 people per year) is a bit higher the death rate (7 per 1000 people per year).
3) Previously the population was growing so quickly that the government introduced strategies such as the '<u>one child policy</u>' to limit the number of children families had.
4) As a result, China now has a <u>middle-aged population</u> — there are lots more people aged 40-55 than there are aged 0-15.
5) China is an <u>Newly Industrialised Country</u> (NIC) with a fairly high level of development.
   - The average <u>life expectancy</u> for babies born today is <u>75 years</u>.
   - The <u>literacy rate</u> is <u>95%</u>.

See page 5 for more about NICs.

Half the population live in **Cities**

1) In China, <u>51%</u> of the population live in <u>urban areas</u>.
2) There is a <u>high rate</u> of <u>migration</u> from <u>rural areas</u> to <u>cities</u>, so urban areas are growing.
3) The <u>three largest cities</u> by population in China are Shanghai, Beijing and Zhoukou (see previous page). Many cities have <u>expanded</u> until they <u>join up</u> and become continuous urban areas with even larger populations.
4) As a result, urban areas like the <u>Yangtze River Delta</u> (which includes Shanghai) have very high population densities.
5) In <u>rural</u> areas, settlements are typically <u>compact villages</u> of <u>mud</u> or <u>sun-dried brick</u> houses. But there is a <u>great variety</u> of settlement type across China.

China has a **Very Large Economy**

1) The government in China <u>owns</u> lots of the businesses and controls what companies are <u>allowed</u> to sell or do. This has been <u>relaxed</u> a lot in some places though, e.g. the <u>Shanghai Free Trade Zone</u> where <u>global businesses</u> may trade with fewer restrictions.
2) China has a very large <u>manufacturing industry</u> and is now the world's <u>largest exporter</u> of goods to other countries. Manufacturing, mining and construction are <u>growing rapidly</u>.
3) <u>Agriculture</u> is also a very important part of China's economy. There are about <u>350 million people</u> employed in farming in China. It is the world's largest producer of rice.
4) China is the world's <u>second-largest economy</u> by total GNI. The wealth is divided between a lot of people though, so China's <u>GNI per head</u> is only fairly high at <u>5720 US Dollars</u>.
5) <u>Some parts</u> of China have a much higher GNI per head though, e.g. in Hong Kong (where special rules on business apply), GNI per head is 36 560 US Dollars.

China is an enormous country that's still growing

It's <u>40</u> times bigger than the <u>UK</u> with <u>20</u> times the number of people. And the population and economy are <u>still growing</u>. It's definitely a country worth learning about.

Russia

Confusingly, the western part of Russia counts as part of <u>Europe</u>, and the eastern bit is in <u>Asia</u>.

Moscow *is the* Capital *of* Russia

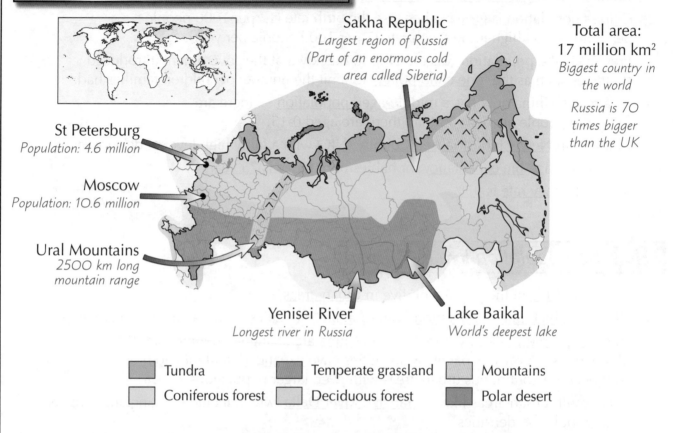

Sakha Republic
*Largest region of Russia
(Part of an enormous cold
area called Siberia)*

Total area:
17 million km²
*Biggest country in
the world*

*Russia is 70
times bigger
than the UK*

St Petersburg
Population: 4.6 million

Moscow
Population: 10.6 million

Ural Mountains
*2500 km long
mountain range*

Yenisei River
Longest river in Russia

Lake Baikal
World's deepest lake

Tundra	Temperate grassland	Mountains
Coniferous forest	Deciduous forest	Polar desert

Russia has Lots *of* Tundra *and* Coniferous Forest

The biggest country on Earth has a lot of different biomes. There is <u>temperate grassland</u> and <u>deciduous forest</u> in the south, <u>coniferous forest</u> in the middle and <u>tundra</u> in the north.

1) Coniferous forests cover most of the middle of Russia.

- The area is <u>cold</u> — temperatures in winter may be as low as <u>–30 °C</u>, and the summers are <u>cool</u>.

- <u>Precipitation</u> is <u>low</u> because there isn't much water in the air so far from the sea.

- Most trees are <u>coniferous</u> — this means they have <u>needles</u> (to reduce water loss), a <u>conical shape</u> (to let snow slide off) and <u>shallow roots</u> (to survive in frozen ground).

2) Tundra is found in the north of Russia.

- Temperatures are <u>very low</u> in tundra — most of the ground is permanently frozen (<u>permafrost</u>).

- There isn't much <u>precipitation</u>. It usually falls as <u>snow</u>.

- Plants are <u>rarely</u> above <u>30 cm high</u>. Mosses, lichens and grasses are common.

3) Some of the most northern areas are <u>polar deserts</u>. Like hot deserts there is very little precipitation (less than 250 mm each year), but they are much colder.

4) There are also areas of <u>temperate grassland</u>, <u>deciduous forest</u> and <u>mountains</u> (see page 6).

Russia

Russia's *Population* is *Declining* and *Ageing*

1) The population of Russia is about 142 million people.

2) Russia's population is declining because the birth rate (12 per 1000 people per year) is lower than the death rate (14 per 1000 people per year).

3) The population of Russia is ageing — there are more older people than young people. Only 16% of the population are aged under 15.

4) Russia is a developed country, but it's not as developed as the UK or the USA.
   - The average life expectancy at birth is 70 years — this is quite low. The life expectancy for men is much lower than women — just 64 years.
   - The literacy rate is 99.7% — this is very high.

Population Density is very *Low*

1) On average, Russia's population density is 8.4 people per km^2. This is one of the lowest population densities in the world.

2) Although Russia has some very large, densely populated cities like Moscow, large parts of the country like the Sakha Republic in Siberia (0.3 people per km^2) are almost completely uninhabited.

3) The majority of Russians live in towns and cities — 74% live in urban areas.

4) The largest and most heavily populated cities (Moscow and St Petersburg), are located in the very west of the country near the border with Europe.

Russia produces a lot of *Oil*, *Gas* and *Metals*

1) Russia has very large reserves of raw materials. These make up a large proportion of Russia's economic activities.

2) Fossil fuel production is a major industry. Russia produces about 20% of the world's total oil supply and 25% of the world's gas. Some of this is exported to European countries.

3) Russia produces significant quantities of metals like iron ore and has the world's largest forest reserves.

4) There are large manufacturing and services industries. 62% of jobs in Russia are in the services sector.

5) GNI per head is quite high at 12 700 US Dollars. This wealth is quite unevenly distributed though, with a few people (referred to as 'oligarchs') becoming very wealthy billionaires over the last 20-30 years.

6) Russia used to be part of the USSR, a very powerful communist state. Today it is a democracy with regular elections.

Russia — it's big, but lots of it is cold and empty

Just because some large bits of Russia have almost nobody living there doesn't mean it's not important to know about. It's an enormous country with a population more than twice the size of the UK, and it's full of useful natural resources like oil and gas and trees.

The Middle East

The 'Middle East' is a bit of a <u>vague term</u>. You might see maps of the area that include a slightly different selection of countries, but these are the places it usually refers to.

The *Middle East* is made up of *Several Countries*

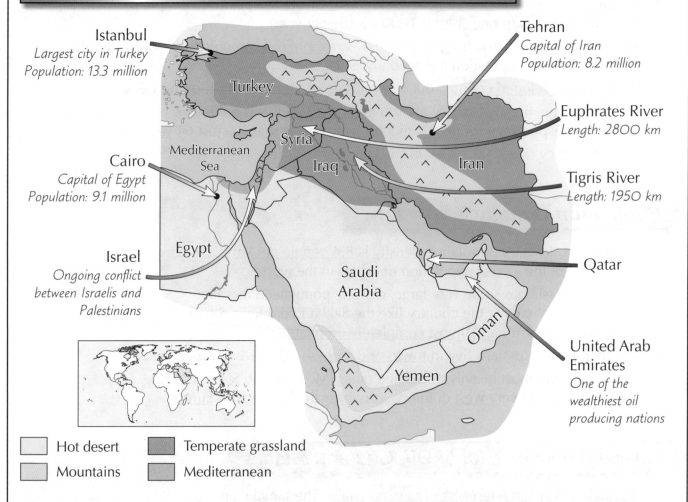

Istanbul
Largest city in Turkey
Population: 13.3 million

Tehran
Capital of Iran
Population: 8.2 million

Euphrates River
Length: 2800 km

Cairo
Capital of Egypt
Population: 9.1 million

Tigris River
Length: 1950 km

Israel
Ongoing conflict
between Israelis and
Palestinians

Qatar

United Arab
Emirates
One of the
wealthiest oil
producing nations

Turkey
Syria
Mediterranean Sea
Iraq
Iran
Egypt
Saudi Arabia
Oman
Yemen

	Hot desert		Temperate grassland
	Mountains		Mediterranean

Much of the *Middle East* is *Hot Desert*, a bit is *Mediterranean*

Large parts of the Middle East are <u>hot</u> with <u>low precipitation</u> — a desert climate. But there are also areas of <u>temperate grassland</u> and a nice bit of <u>Mediterranean biome</u> on the coast.

1) Large parts of the Middle East, including all of Saudi Arabia, are <u>hot desert</u> (see page 2).

   - Temperatures are <u>high</u> and precipitation is <u>low</u> in Middle Eastern deserts. In Muscat (capital of Oman), the <u>average annual temperature</u> is over <u>28 °C</u> and there is only <u>100 mm</u> of precipitation each year.

   - Not much can <u>grow naturally</u> in Saudi Arabia — only small shrubs and herbs can survive the high temperatures, lack of water and the poor, sandy soil.

2) The Mediterranean biome is found all around the <u>coast</u> of the <u>Mediterranean Sea</u>.

   - <u>Summers</u> are <u>hot</u> (up to 30 °C monthly average) and <u>winters</u> are <u>warm</u>, rarely dropping below 5 °C.

   - Almost all the annual <u>precipitation</u> occurs in <u>winter months</u>. Summers are very dry.

   - <u>Evergreen</u> and <u>deciduous</u> trees are the natural vegetation of Mediterranean regions. This vegetation is often replaced by <u>thorny shrubs</u> due to overgrazing and cultivation.

3) Some areas such as inland Turkey and Iran are <u>temperate grassland</u> — see page 6 for more.

The Middle East

Oil is a Big Part of many Middle Eastern Economies

1) Many countries in the Middle East have very large reserves of <u>oil</u> and <u>natural gas</u> that is exported <u>worldwide</u>, including to Europe.

2) Oil and gas make up about <u>half</u> of <u>Qatar's economy</u>. Much of it is exported, generating a very <u>large income</u> — Qatar's GNI per head is 74 600 US Dollars, one of the highest in the world.

3) It's not just oil though — <u>Israel</u> has a significant <u>science</u> and <u>technology sector</u>. <u>Agriculture</u> and <u>manufacturing</u> represent a large part of <u>Turkey's economy</u>.

4) <u>Development</u> varies across the Middle East. Countries like <u>Israel</u> have a <u>high</u> level of development — <u>life expectancy</u> at birth is <u>81 years</u> and the <u>literacy rate</u> is <u>97%</u>.

5) A few countries have a low level of development. Life expectancy in <u>Yemen</u> is only <u>65 years</u>, and the literacy rate is <u>65%</u>.

6) There have been several <u>conflicts</u> in the Middle East, some still ongoing. Events like the <u>Iraq War</u> (2003-2011) and the ongoing conflict in Israel can cause major <u>disruption</u> to levels of <u>development</u> as well as loss of life.

Population Size and Characteristics Vary across the Middle East

1) The Middle East is made up of very different countries with very different populations.
   - <u>Egypt</u> has the <u>largest population</u> in the Middle East — <u>86.9 million</u> people live there. <u>Cyprus</u> has the <u>smallest</u> population — just <u>1.2 million</u> people live on the island.
   - <u>Yemen</u> has the <u>youngest</u> population. <u>42%</u> of the population are <u>under 15 years old</u>. <u>Qatar</u> has the <u>oldest</u> population — just <u>13%</u> of the population are under 15 years old (due to large numbers of foreign male migrants coming to Qatar looking for work).

2) Population <u>growth rates</u> have been affected by high rates of <u>migration</u> during <u>conflicts</u>. E.g. in one year during Syria's civil war, the population of Syria <u>fell</u> by around <u>10%</u> while neighbouring Lebanon <u>grew</u> by around <u>9%</u>.

3) Population <u>density</u> varies across the Middle East.
   - In <u>Bahrain</u> (a very small, densely populated island nation) there are <u>1859 people per km²</u>.
   - <u>Oman</u> (a country with large areas of empty desert) has the <u>lowest</u> population density in the Middle East — just <u>10 people per km²</u>.

4) The proportion of people living in rural areas compared to towns and cities varies too.
   - In Qatar, <u>99%</u> of people live in <u>urban areas</u>.
   - <u>32%</u> of people in Yemen live in an <u>urban area</u>.

Oil and (sadly) conflict are really significant in the Middle East

The important thing here is that the 'Middle East' <u>isn't just one place</u>. It's a mix of countries with different climates, populations and industries that <u>share</u> some <u>characteristics</u> and not others. So don't go thinking you can learn a few things about one country and call it a day.

Questions

Phew, there was a lot of information in that section. So many places to know about.
These questions will check you've taken it all in — if you can't remember something,
go back and learn it again until you can ace all these questions.

Warm-up Questions

1) Name the seven continents.

2) Name two biomes that are found in Africa.

3) What is Gross National Income per head?

4) Name two countries which have tropical rainforest vegetation.

5) Give an example of a Newly Industrialised Country.

6) What is the world's most highly populated country?

7) Where in Russia is tundra found?

8) Name three countries in the Middle East.

Practice Questions

It's practice question time. They're a bit harder than the warm-up questions, so take it steady.

1) The map below shows the world divided into biomes.

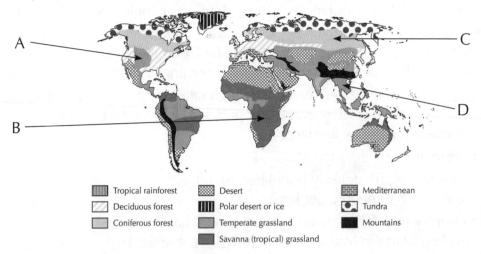

||||| Tropical rainforest		Desert		Mediterranean
//// Deciduous forest		|||| Polar desert or ice		Tundra
Coniferous forest		Temperate grassland		Mountains
		Savanna (tropical) grassland		

a) Which biome does each arrow above point to?

b) Copy out the following passage, using the correct word from each pair.

A biome is an area with (**distinctive / ordinary**) climate and vegetation. Biomes usually
cover a (**small / large**) area, often spanning (**multiple countries / a few kilometres**).
The United Kingdom is in an area of (**coniferous forest / deciduous forest**).

c) Give one example of a biome and describe where it can be found.

Questions

Just a few more questions to go before you're nearly done with section one...

2) Most of Africa south of the Sahara Desert is savanna grassland.

   a) Describe the climate of savanna grassland areas in Africa.

   b) Give one way that plants are adapted to the conditions in savanna grassland.

3) Copy and complete the table using the words below.

Egypt   **39%**   **74 years**   **74%**   **Ethiopia**   **61 years**

Level of Development	Country	Life Expectancy	Literary Rate
Lower			
Higher			

4) Which of these boxes best describes the tropical rainforest biome in India?

   ① Temperature: 26 – 28 °C
      Precipitation: over 2000 mm each year
      Seasons: hot and wet all year round

   ② Temperature: up to 16 °C
      Precipitation: 500 – 900 mm each year
      Seasons: mild summers, cold winters

5) Which of the following statements are true?

   a) China is the largest country in the world by area.

   b) China is the largest country in the world by population.

   c) Beijing is the most highly populated city in China.

   d) Almost all people in China live in rural areas.

   e) China has a middle-aged population.

6) Write down the Middle Eastern countries that the arrows are pointing to.

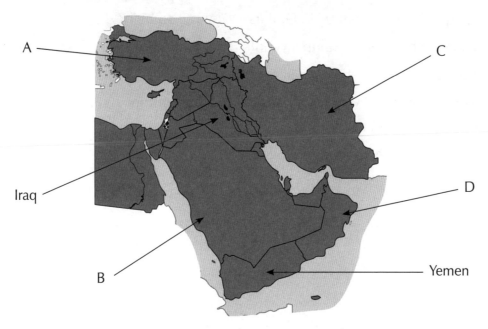

Section One — Summary Questions

Section one is all about locational knowledge — places in our world that you need to know about. It's all jolly useful background knowledge for some of the geographical concepts you'll come across in the rest of this book. And knowing where these continents and countries are might just save you from an embarrassing mistake later in life...

1) What is a continent?

2) What are desert, savanna, temperate deciduous forest and tundra all examples of?

3) True or false: Africa is a large country.

4) Which is closest to the Sahara Desert's annual rainfall — 20 mm or 950 mm?

5) How many people are there in Africa?

6) What do the locations of Cairo, Kampala and Algiers have in common?

7) Which continent is India in?

8) Why do plants in rainforests have thick, waxy pointed leaves?

9) Which part of the economy do half of all Indians work in?

10) Is India getting poorer or wealthier? What indicator can be used to measure this?

11) What sort of biome covers the Tibetan Plateau?

12) What is the biggest country in the world by area?

13) How are the trees in coniferous forest areas adapted to conditions in northern Russia?

14) What does 'permafrost' mean?

15) Is Russia's population growing, staying constant or declining?

16) Describe Russia's population density. How does it vary across Russia?

17) Russia produces 25% of the world's global supply of which energy resource?

18) Where in the Middle East can the Mediterranean biome be found?

19) Describe the Mediterranean biome.

20) Qatar's GNI per head is 74 600 US Dollars. Why is it so high?

21) Give an example of a country in the Middle East with a low level of development.

22) What caused Syria's population to fall by around 10% in a year?

23) Name one country in the Middle East with a high proportion
of people living in urban areas.

24) Name one country in the Middle East with a low proportion
of people living in urban areas.

The Geological Timescale

The Earth is so <u>old</u> that you can't measure its history using human timescales — that's where the <u>geological timescale</u> comes in.

The *Geological Timescale* shows *events* in the *Earth's history*

1) The <u>geological timescale</u> divides the Earth's <u>history</u> into different <u>categories</u> called <u>geological periods</u>.

2) A <u>geological period</u> is a period of time when events, such as the formation of certain types of rock, happened.

3) The table below shows all the <u>most recent geological periods</u> (you don't need to learn their names).

These are the major periods when each of these rocks formed — some of them formed at other times too.

Chalk formed in the UK when warm tropical seas covered much of the land.

Geological Period	Began, million years before present
Quaternary	2.6
Tertiary	65
Cretaceous	145
Jurassic	215
Triassic	245
Permian	285
Carboniferous	360
Devonian	410
Silurian	440
Ordovician	505
Cambrian	585

Clay formed in the UK under warm and humid conditions.

Carboniferous limestone formed in the UK under tropical conditions.

Granite formed in the UK under volcanic conditions.

4) It takes a <u>very long time</u> for rocks to <u>form</u>.

5) The rocks found in the UK <u>today</u> were all formed <u>many millions</u> of years ago, when the climate in the UK was very different to how it is today.

6) <u>Humans</u> have only been around for the last <u>200 000 years</u>, and it's thought that the Earth is <u>4 600 000 000 years old</u>, so geological time is on a totally <u>different timescale</u> to <u>human time</u>.

The Earth's history is divided up using the geological timescale

So, the geological timescale lists geological periods in history. Different rocks were formed during each of these periods, and the UK had a very different climate to what we have today.

The Tectonic Jigsaw

The Earth's crust is made of huge floating <u>plates</u> — you need to <u>understand</u> it if you're going to get anywhere with <u>tectonics</u>.

The **Earth's Crust** is divided up into **Plates**

1) <u>Plates</u> sit on top of the <u>mantle</u> (the semi-molten rock inside the Earth). They move very slowly (a few mm per year). This movement is caused by <u>convection currents</u> in the mantle.

2) The places where plates meet are called <u>plate boundaries</u> or <u>margins</u>.

There are **Three** types of plate boundary

1 When two plates diverge (move apart), a <u>constructive</u> plate boundary is formed. Magma (liquid rock) rises from the gap created and cools, forming new crustal rocks.

An example of this type is the <u>Mid-Atlantic Ridge</u>, which runs north to south along the middle of the Atlantic Ocean, separating America from Africa and Europe.

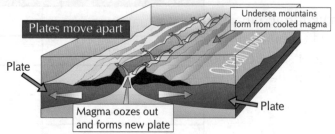

Plates move apart

Undersea mountains form from cooled magma

Plate

Plate

Magma oozes out and forms new plate

2 When two plates push against each other, you get a <u>destructive</u> plate boundary. This often causes one plate to be forced down and the other plate to squash up. The squashed up plate (and sediments from on top of the plate) build up to form <u>fold mountains</u>. Earthquakes and volcanoes are common.

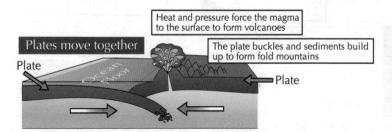

Heat and pressure force the magma to the surface to form volcanoes

Plates move together

The plate buckles and sediments build up to form fold mountains

Plate

Plate

An example of this occurs down the <u>west coast of South America</u> — this is how the Andes Mountains were formed.

3 Sometimes plates slide sideways against each other — these are called <u>conservative</u> plate margins. Volcanoes are rare but earthquakes are common with this type.

The <u>San Andreas Fault in California</u> on the west coast of North America is a good example of this.

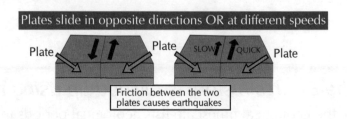

Plates slide in opposite directions OR at different speeds

Plate

Plate

SLOW QUICK Plate

Friction between the two plates causes earthquakes

The Tectonic Jigsaw

*Volcanoes and earthquakes are **Near** plate margins*

The two maps below show the plate boundaries and where volcanoes, earthquakes and fold mountains are found. See how they match up.

Plate Boundaries and Direction of plate Movement

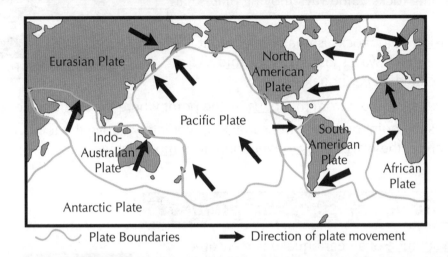

Plate Boundaries ⌇ Direction of plate movement ➙

> *There are over 600 active volcanoes in the world today — the greatest concentration is around the Pacific Ocean in the 'Ring of Fire'.*

Volcano, Earthquake and Fold Mountain zones

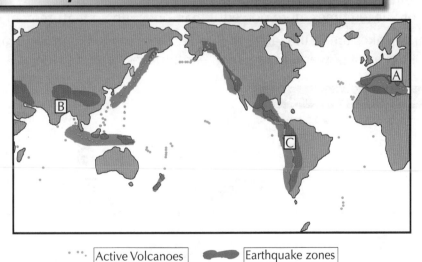

⸱⸱⸱ Active Volcanoes ▬ Earthquake zones

A: Alps, B: Himalayas, C: Andes Fold Mountains

Plate movements are small and slow, but the effects can be huge

So it's quite simple really — volcanoes, fold mountains and earthquakes all occur at plate boundaries because they're caused by plates moving against or away from each other.

Earthquakes

Floating plates don't sound too harmful. But when the plates come together you can get earthquakes...

Earthquakes occur at Destructive or Conservative plate margins

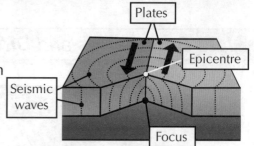

1) As two plates move towards each other, one can be pushed down under the other one and into the mantle. If this plate gets stuck it causes a lot of strain in the surrounding rocks. Sideways-moving plates can also get stuck.

2) When this tension in the rocks is finally released it produces strong shock waves known as seismic waves. This is called an earthquake.

3) The shock waves spread out from the focus — the point where the earthquake starts.

4) The epicentre is the point on the Earth's surface immediately above the focus. Near the epicentre, the waves are stronger and cause more damage.

The Richter Scale measures Earthquakes

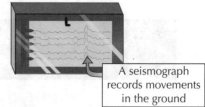

A seismograph records movements in the ground

1) The size or magnitude of an earthquake is measured using a seismometer; a machine with a seismograph on a revolving drum. Earthquake vibrations are recorded by a sensitive arm with a pen at the end which moves up and down.

2) These readings are measured using the Richter Scale for energy released, which is an open-ended scale (it goes on forever).

3) This is a logarithmic scale — which means that an earthquake with a measurement of 5 is ten times more powerful than one with a measurement of 4.

4) Most serious earthquakes are in the range of 5 to 9. The earthquake in San Francisco in 1906 was one of the most powerfully recorded earthquakes, with a value of 8.6.

The Richter Scale and Possible effects

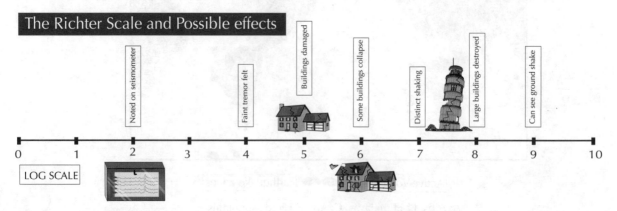

Make sure you know what a focus and an epicentre are

Don't forget — the Richter Scale goes on forever, but there's never been a measurement above 10. And remember that the damage an earthquake causes isn't just because of its size — it also depends on where it hit and how strong or weak the buildings there are.

Volcanoes

Volcanoes are often (but not always) <u>cone shaped</u>. They are formed by material from the <u>mantle</u> being forced through an opening in the Earth's crust, the <u>vent</u>.

Volcanoes are *Extinct*, *Dormant* or *Active*

1) <u>EXTINCT</u>: It will never erupt again.
   E.g. <u>Devil's Tower, Wyoming</u>.

2) <u>DORMANT</u>: It hasn't erupted in 2000 years.

3) <u>ACTIVE</u>: It has erupted recently and is likely
   to erupt again. E.g. <u>Mt. Etna</u> in Sicily is Europe's
   most active volcano.

Other Major Active Volcanoes	
PLACE	MAJOR ERUPTION
Montserrat, Caribbean	1997
Pinatubo, Philippines	1991
Mount St. Helens, USA	1980

A *Composite Volcano* is made up of *Lava* and *Ash*

1) Four different types of substance
   can be ejected through the <u>vent</u>:

   - <u>ash</u>
   - <u>gas</u>
   - pieces of rock known as <u>volcanic bombs</u>
   - molten rock — known as <u>magma</u>
     when it's under the ground and <u>lava</u>
     when it reaches the surface

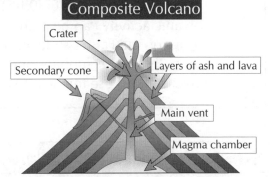

Composite Volcano

Crater · Secondary cone · Layers of ash and lava · Main vent · Magma chamber

2) Once this material has been thrown out at the surface, it <u>cools</u> and <u>hardens</u>, forming the volcano mountain from the mixture of ash and lava.

3) <u>Mount Etna</u> in Sicily is a famous composite volcano.

Shield and *Dome* volcanoes are made of *Lava Only*

Volcanoes made up just from hardened lava are known as one of these two types:

1) <u>Shield volcanoes</u>: where the lava is <u>alkaline</u> and <u>runny</u>. It flows quickly and easily, spreading over large areas forming <u>wide</u>, <u>flatter features</u> — e.g. <u>Mauna Loa</u> (Hawaiian Islands).

2) <u>Dome volcanoes</u>: where the lava is <u>acid</u> and <u>thicker</u>. It flows more slowly and hardens quickly to form <u>steep-sided features</u> — e.g. <u>Mt. St. Helens</u> (USA).

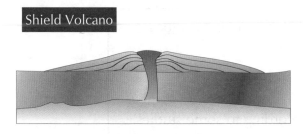

Shield Volcano

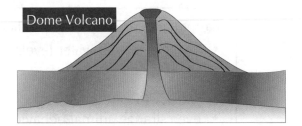

Dome Volcano

Sketch and label a diagram of composite volcanoes

These volcanoes shouldn't cause you much trouble to learn — just remember the <u>three types</u>.
Scribble a mini-essay on how <u>composite</u> volcanoes, <u>shield</u> and <u>dome</u> volcanoes are formed.

Surviving Tectonic Hazards

As well as thinking about how earthquakes and volcanic eruptions (often called 'tectonic hazards') occur, you need to think about how the hazards affect people, and how people try to cope with the dangers.

People live in *Earthquake* and *Volcanic Zones*

1) Volcanic lava and ash make fertile soils so people settle and farm nearby.

2) Precious minerals and fossil fuels are found in volcanic zones.

3) Land is cheap in volcanic and earthquake zones and people feel safer with technological advances like 'earthquake proof' houses.

4) Studies have shown that lots of people are living in earthquake zones — so many that it would be extremely difficult to re-house them, and many of them don't want to leave anyway.

5) Volcanic activity can heat underground water, forming hot-water springs on the Earth's surface. This water can be used for heating houses, hot water supplies and producing electricity (geothermal power stations use the heat to drive turbines that create electricity).

Scientists try to *Predict* hazards in advance

So as it's not practical to move everyone away, there need to be ways of reducing the dangers for all the people living in these areas. One way is to spot the problem before it happens...

Scientists monitor the tell-tale signs that go before a volcanic eruption. These clues include things like:
- lots of tiny earthquakes
- rising magma detected under the Earth's surface
- escaping gas
- increased magma temperature
- changes in tilt of the volcano sides.

Earthquakes are harder to predict but there are some clues...
- changes in well water levels
- gas emissions
- cracks appearing in rocks
- even strange animal behaviour according to some studies...

Volcanic zones are quite nice places to live... most of the time

This is what makes predicting volcanic eruptions and monitoring earthquakes so important. It's pretty incredible how people cope living where earthquakes or eruptions are likely.

Surviving Tectonic Hazards

Good Planning *reduces the effects of a hazard*

1) MONITORING helps <u>predict</u> when hazards are coming so people can be <u>warned</u>.

2) FAMILIES can organise <u>supplies</u> of food and water rations, dust masks, spare clothes, basic medical supplies, shelters, torches, batteries, mobile phones and other useful stuff.

3) LOCAL EMERGENCY SERVICES such as the police, fire brigade and ambulance service can be well <u>prepared</u> to deal with any hazard.

4) DISASTER PLANS can be drawn up by <u>local authorities</u> and <u>governments</u> and practised in order to help reduce damage, death and injury (e.g. how to get a lot of people away from a volcano very quickly).

5) INFORMATION on emergency <u>procedures</u> can be made available to the public — e.g. in school classes, meetings for adults, pamphlets, newspaper adverts etc. Simply sheltering under a table or avoiding standing next to walls can save someone's life.

6) EMERGENCY SUPPLIES of <u>water</u> and <u>power</u> can be organised in advance.

Large computer-controlled concrete counterweight moves in opposite way to earthquake.

Cross-bracings allow more flexibility.

Rubber shock absorbers in foundations.

7) BUILDING AND ROAD DESIGNS can be <u>planned</u> for earth movements, so they don't collapse under the strain. E.g. new <u>skyscrapers</u> in earthquake zones can be built with a computer-controlled counterweight, cross-bracings and special foundations to reduce the impact of an earthquake.

8) STRENGTHENED ROADS AND RAILWAYS can help <u>reduce</u> damage. Sometimes this doesn't work, e.g. in Japan, the 1995 Kobe earthquake unexpectedly bent the track of the Bullet train.

Preparation and warning are essential in hazard zones

Scribble a list of things that can be done to <u>prepare</u> for a tectonic hazard.
Then jot a quick paragraph on the reasons <u>why</u> people live in hazard zones.

Tectonic Hazards in LEDCs and MEDCs

Earthquakes and volcanoes are a nightmare anywhere, but they cause <u>more problems for LEDCs</u>.

MEDC stands for More Economically Developed Country and LEDC stands for Less Economically Developed Country.

Three *factors affect* how serious *the disaster is*

1 <u>RURAL / URBAN AREAS</u>: Rural areas have fewer people and buildings so the size of the disaster is smaller.

2 <u>POPULATION DENSITY</u>: Pretty obvious really, the more people, the more deaths. E.g. the Indian earthquake in 2001 occurred in a densely populated area. It resulted in 20 000 deaths.

3 <u>HOW PREPARED COUNTRIES ARE</u>: How ready a country is depends on how developed it is. Less Economically Developed Countries (LEDCs) have less time, money and expertise to prepare for hazards. More Economically Developed Countries (MEDCs) are better prepared but they still can't stop disasters happening. They can just limit the damage.

MEDCs *can put* Emergency Plans *into action*

1) Local authority <u>experts</u> assess the seriousness of the situation and the damage.
2) Local <u>citizens</u> should be kept <u>informed</u> — they need to be reassured and told what to do next.
3) <u>Immediate emergencies</u> must be dealt with <u>first</u>. All casualties should be taken to hospital and fires must be put out — fires are a big problem if gas pipes have been damaged.
4) <u>Disrupted public services</u> such as power, water supply and sewage disposal must be <u>restored</u> as soon as possible because there is a risk of <u>disease</u>.
5) <u>Communication networks</u> such as roads, bridges, railways and telephones may have been damaged and <u>mending</u> these is top priority so that <u>help</u> from outside the area can get in.
6) The efforts of <u>individuals</u>, <u>government</u> and <u>NGOs</u> (Non-Governmental Organisations) such as <u>Oxfam</u> and <u>Cafod</u> must be coordinated.
7) Once the situation is <u>clear</u>, and there's <u>no risk</u> of a further hazard, life can get back to normal.

Tectonic hazards can't be stopped

But things can be done to limit damage. Being well-prepared can have a huge impact on the seriousness of a disaster. MEDCs now have comparatively well developed ways of coping.

Tectonic Hazards in LEDCs and MEDCs

LEDCs are not so well prepared...

1) Many people in <u>LEDC hazard zones</u> haven't been given information about what to do if there is a hazard.
2) Some LEDCs <u>don't</u> prepare plans — the government has enough problems already.
3) <u>Communication</u> is bad — many people live in <u>shanty towns</u> with no proper <u>access</u> roads and <u>badly built</u> housing which collapses easily, causing more injury.

...and getting back to normal takes longer

1) There are <u>few experts</u> available to <u>assess</u> the situation.
2) <u>Without plans</u> there will be <u>delays</u> dealing with the fires, injured people, etc.
3) <u>Badly built</u> housing means <u>more damage</u> and allows <u>fires</u> and <u>diseases</u> to spread quickly.
4) <u>Limited communications</u> mean people still don't know what's happening. There will also only be a few ambulances and fire engines available.
5) <u>Water</u> and <u>power supplies</u> are normally <u>poor</u> and mending them is difficult.
6) <u>Roads and transport systems</u> are poor to start with, so it's <u>difficult</u> to bring in supplies of food, medicine, clothes, shelter etc., even if these are available.
7) <u>Shortage of money</u> means they have to rely on <u>foreign aid</u> which takes <u>time</u> to reach them.
8) <u>Medical facilities</u> are <u>limited</u> so many people die of <u>injuries</u> or <u>diseases</u> linked to dirty water supply and poor living conditions.

Questions

It's time to take a break from studying and see how much you've taken in so far. First, have a go at these quick questions to make sure you've been awake through the last 9 pages.

Warm-up Questions

1) Give an example of a conservative plate margin. ✓ Pg 16

2) What are fold mountains? How are they formed?

3) When studying earthquakes what are: the focus, the epicentre, seismic waves?

4) What are extinct and active volcanoes? Give one example of each.

5) What do MEDC and LEDC stand for?

Practice Questions

Now that you're fully warmed up, work your way through these practice questions which will test your knowledge of the previous section in a bit more detail.

1) Copy out the paragraph below using the correct words.

It takes a very (**short / long**) time for rocks to form. The rocks found in the UK today were all formed many (**millions / thousands**) of years ago. The geological timescale divides the Earth's (**atmosphere / history**) into different categories called geological (**periods / types**). Geological time is on a much (**smaller / larger**) scale than human time.

2) Copy and complete this table.

	Direction plates are moving	Type of boundary	Example

3) Are the statements below about tectonic plates true or false?

a) North and South America both share the same plate.

b) The Eurasian and Pacific plates are moving towards each other.

c) Earthquakes and volcanoes are never found at the edges of plates.

Questions

Keep going, five questions to go...

4) Match up the key terms to their definitions.

Focus	A system used to measure the size of earthquakes.
Epicentre	An instrument which detects vibrations.
Richter scale	The point on the earth's surface above the focus, where the effect is strongest.
Seismometer	The point, usually below the surface of the earth, where an earthquake starts.

5) Write a definition for each of the three volcano-related words below.

   a) Extinct   b) Dormant   c) Active

6) Copy the table and fit the sketches, materials and examples into the right places.

   Sketches:

   Materials: *Runny, alkaline lava*   *Lava and ash*   *Thick, acid lava*

   Examples: *Mauna Loa, Hawaii*   *Mt. Etna*   *Mt. St. Helens*

	Shield	Dome	Composite
Sketch			
Made from			
Example			

7) Copy out the paragraph below using the correct words.

   As two (**tectonic / volcanic**) plates move towards each other, they are said to
   (**jump / collide**). The (**water / rock**) between these two plates is pushed up,
   buckling and turning into (**mountains / glaciers**). These (**mountain / valley**)
   ranges are often very (**high / low**) with (**gentle / steep**) slopes.

8) Living near tectonic activity can be dangerous, but there are some benefits.
   Decide whether the advantages below are true or false.

   a) Crops grow quickly and have high yields.

   b) Some of the gases released have important health benefits.

   c) Geothermal energy can be used to generate electricity.

   d) Hot springs can be used for heating and hot water.

Section Two — Summary Questions

A tough section this — lots of fancy terms and ideas to remember. Test yourself NOW on this section because if you leave it till the end you'll get revision-brain-melt-down. These questions will find out if you know your stuff. Do your best — then go and check the pages for the ones you found hard. Don't stress if you can't get them all first time. Just go over the pages and come back to the questions again.

1) Is the following statement true or false?
   Humans were around before most types of rock formed in the UK.

2) What is a geological period?

3) The Earth's crust is divided into plates. What are the places where they meet called?

4) What causes the plates to move?

5) How quickly do plates move? Pick the right answer:
   a) a few metres a year,   b) a few millimetres per year.

6) Draw and label a plate margin with diverging plates and explain what's happening.

7) What type of plate margin is caused by plates moving towards each other? Give an example.

8) Draw and label a destructive plate margin and explain what's happening.

9) Draw and label a conservative plate margin and explain what's happening.

10) Name examples of two plates and two ranges of fold mountains.

11) Where is the main volcano zone in the world and what's it called? [CLUE: BURNING CIRCLE]

12) Where do most earthquakes occur on the Earth's crust and why?

13) How much bigger is a 6-point earthquake than a 5-pointer on the Richter scale?

14) What is a volcano?

15) What is a composite volcano made up of? Name one example.

16) What are the pieces of rock called that fly out of an erupting volcano?

17) What is the difference between lava and magma?

18) Draw a diagram of a composite volcano. Label the vent, crater, magma, ash and lava.

19) Shield and dome volcanoes are both made of lava. How do they differ in shape and composition? Name an example of each.

20) Give four reasons why people live near volcanoes or earthquakes.

21) What do scientists look for to judge whether a volcano is about to erupt?

22) What do they look out for to predict earthquakes?

23) What scientific instrument is used to record movements in the ground?

24) Explain eight ways that the risk of damage in an earthquake zone can be reduced.

25) What are the three main factors that affect the seriousness of a tectonic hazard?

26) Write a short account describing how MEDCs deal with a disaster.

27) Write a mini-essay describing the problems LEDCs have when there's a tectonic disaster.

Types of Rock

Rocks are classed as igneous, sedimentary or metamorphic, depending on how they were formed.

Igneous rocks are formed from Magma

1) EXTRUSIVE igneous rocks are formed when magma spills out on to the surface and cools there (e.g. volcanic rocks). They have a fine texture (e.g. basalt).

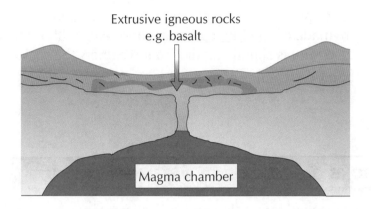

Extrusive igneous rocks
e.g. basalt

Magma chamber

When the magma cools very slowly, large hexagonal columns form — e.g. the Giant's Causeway in Northern Ireland.

hexagonal black columns

2) INTRUSIVE igneous rocks like granite occur when magma cools very slowly before reaching the surface. They have a coarse texture and form features like big domes of rock called batholiths (magma chambers that have cooled slowly and then been exposed by erosion) and tors (see below).

Intrusive igneous rocks
e.g. granite

Surrounding rock has been worn away

batholith

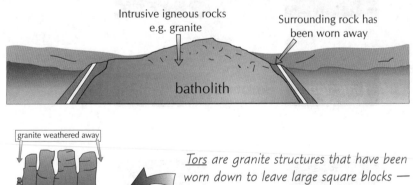

granite weathered away

Tors are granite structures that have been worn down to leave large square blocks — e.g. the tors on Dartmoor.

Extrusive rock cools outside the surface, intrusive rock cools inside

The way that igneous rock is formed affects its texture and shape. Learn the different processes that create these rocks, the examples and the structures extrusive and intrusive rocks produce.

Types of Rock

Sedimentary Rocks are formed from Particles

1) Sandstones, shales and clays are made from tiny particles of sand or clay eroded from past landscapes by wind or water and deposited in layers, e.g. in the sea. Later they're uplifted to a position above sea-level. These layers of rock are called beds or strata and they're separated by bedding planes.

2) Limestone and chalk are formed from the remains of tiny shells and micro-skeletons. They're made of calcium carbonate and react with dilute acid. All rainwater (not just acid rain) is slightly acidic, so it weathers the rocks.

3) Coal is made from carbon rich remains of tropical plants.

Metamorphic Rocks are formed by Heat or Pressure

'Metamorphic' just means 'changed form'. Igneous or sedimentary rocks can be changed by heat from magma or pressure from earth movements. The chemical composition of the rocks stays the same but the new rocks are harder and more compact.

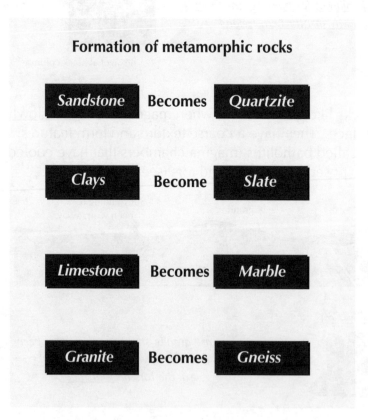

Formation of metamorphic rocks

Sandstone	**Becomes**	*Quartzite*
Clays	**Become**	*Slate*
Limestone	**Becomes**	*Marble*
Granite	**Becomes**	*Gneiss*

Sedimentary rock — it's not as hard as you think

There are a few things to get mixed up here. Don't do it. Make sure you know how sedimentary and metamorphic rocks are formed, their characteristics, and examples.

Weathering

Weathering is the breakdown of rocks by physical, chemical or biological processes — it takes place on site, so there is no movement involved.

Physical weathering Breaks Down rock surfaces

1) Freeze-Thaw action in temperate climates

1) During winter in the British Isles temperatures are below 0°C on many nights but above 0°C during the days.
2) Water gets trapped in cracks in the rock. It expands when it freezes at night, pressurising the sides of the rock.
3) During the day the ice melts and contracts, releasing the pressure on the rock cracks.
4) Alternating expansion and contraction weakens the rock and pieces break off. This is called FROST SHATTERING.
5) If this process happens to rocks at the top of a steep slope it produces scree (piles of rocks) at the foot of the slope.

Water falls in crack

Ice

Block breaks off

2) Onion-Skin Weathering in hot desert climates

1) Hot desert areas have a big daily temperature range (35°C in the day, 10°C at night).
2) Each day, surface layers of rock heat up and expand. At night the cold makes them contract — this causes thin layers to peel off.

DAY

NIGHT

...Later

Heat makes rock surfaces expand, cold makes them contract...

All of this warming up and cooling down can cause bits of rock's to fall off. Make sure you can describe both of the weathering processes on this page clearly, using the proper terms.

Weathering

Plant Roots, Decay and Creatures cause Biological Weathering

1) <u>Plant roots</u> can <u>grow down</u> through cracks in rock surfaces and push them apart, <u>loosening</u> fragments.

2) <u>Decaying plants</u> and <u>animal remains</u> make <u>acids</u> which <u>eat away</u> at the rocks below.

3) <u>Burrowing creatures</u>, e.g. rabbits and worms, break up softer rocks like clay.

Chemical weathering involves Reactions on the rock

1) <u>Limestone areas</u> are weathered when limestone <u>reacts</u> with <u>rainwater</u>, which is a weak <u>acid</u>.

When it rains the limestone rock <u>is dissolved</u> along weaknesses called joints (vertical weaknesses in the rock) and bedding planes (horizontal weaknesses).

This process forms special features called <u>solution features</u>.
Examples of solution features are:

1) <u>Caves</u>

2) <u>Swallow holes</u> — where a river disappears down into the limestone.

3) <u>Clints</u> (blocks of limestone) and <u>grikes</u> (the gaps between the blocks) — which make up a limestone pavement (see the diagram and photograph below).

4) <u>Stalactites</u> and <u>stalagmites</u> — water droplets evaporate, leaving traces of limestone which grow on cave roofs and floors.

Malham in North Yorkshire is a limestone area and it has lots of solution features caused by chemical weathering.

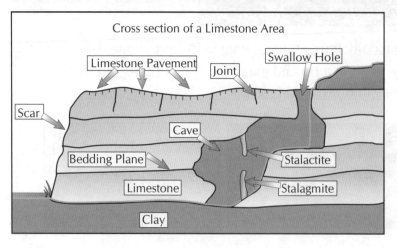

Cross section of a Limestone Area

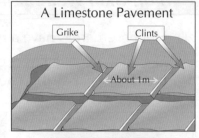

A Limestone Pavement

2) <u>Granite areas</u> react chemically, <u>breaking down</u> to form <u>kaolin</u> or <u>china clay</u>, e.g. in Cornwall.

Make sure you understand all the processes involved in weathering

Remember, you need to understand the way each kind of weathering works. Write down the three types of <u>weathering</u> (physical, biological, chemical), and learn them.

Rocks, Landscapes and People

The <u>features</u> that make up a landscape depend on the type of <u>rock</u>, and the types of <u>weathering</u> and <u>erosion</u>. The landscape determines the <u>land use</u> and land uses cause <u>conflict</u>.

Different Types of rock create *Different Landscapes*

1) *Granite* — *landscape and land use (e.g. Dartmoor)*

1) Granite is <u>resistant</u> to erosion, forming <u>distinctive</u> landscape features like tors and rocky outcrops.
2) Granite is <u>impermeable</u> — which means it doesn't let water soak through. This results in <u>lakes</u> and <u>rivers</u> and lots of <u>marshy areas</u>.
3) <u>Granite</u> weathers to produce <u>poor acidic soil</u>.

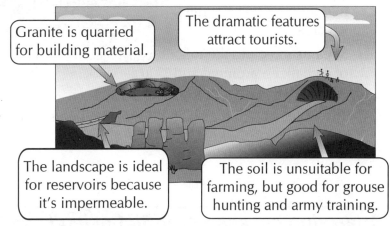

Granite is quarried for building material.

The dramatic features attract tourists.

The landscape is ideal for reservoirs because it's impermeable.

The soil is unsuitable for farming, but good for grouse hunting and army training.

Be careful that you don't get erosion and weathering mixed up: Erosion is where rocks and soil are worn down by movement, e.g. by a river, and the loose material is removed. Weathering is where rocks and soil are broken up or weakened by the weather, and the material stays where it is.

2) *Limestone* — *landscape and land use (e.g. Yorkshire Dales)*

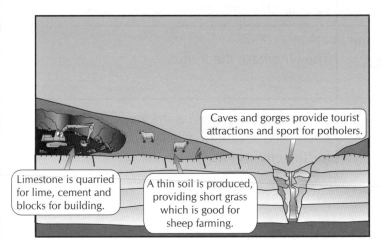

Caves and gorges provide tourist attractions and sport for potholers.

Limestone is quarried for lime, cement and blocks for building.

A thin soil is produced, providing short grass which is good for sheep farming.

1) The landscape produced by <u>limestone</u> is called <u>karst</u> scenery.
2) Limestone produces <u>flat-topped moorlands</u> with steep edges cut into by <u>gorges</u> (steep-sided valleys).
3) Water can't soak into limestone but it does enter it through surface cracks or joints, leaving <u>few surface streams</u>.
4) <u>Settlements</u> are found at the base of hills where the water comes out as <u>springs</u>.

Granite = reservoirs, limestone = caves

Make sure you can <u>describe</u> a granite landscape and a limestone landscape, give the <u>land uses</u> and name an <u>example</u> for each one.

Rocks, Landscapes and People

3) *Chalk — landscape and land use (e.g. South Downs)*

1) <u>Chalk</u> forms <u>escarpments</u> — with <u>scarp</u> (steep) slopes and <u>dip</u> (gentle) slopes.

2) Chalk is <u>porous</u> (full of tiny holes) so rainwater soaks into it, leaving <u>few surface streams</u>.

3) Streams soak into the top of a chalk escarpment and reappear at the bottom as <u>springs</u>.

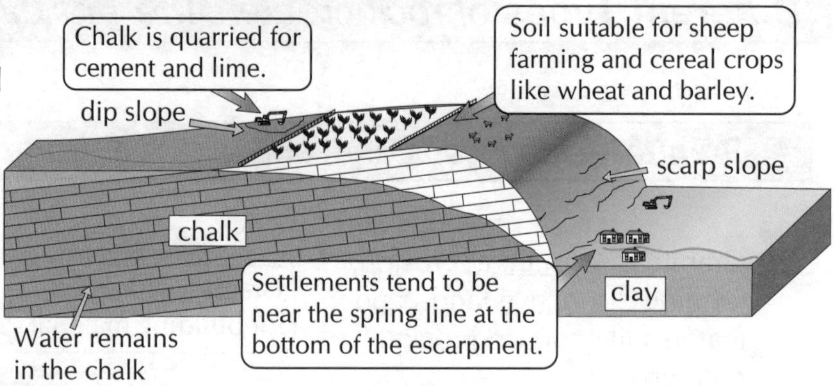

4) The water stored in a chalk hillside can be used as a <u>natural reservoir</u>.

Chalk is quarried for cement and lime.

dip slope

Soil suitable for sheep farming and cereal crops like wheat and barley.

scarp slope

chalk

Settlements tend to be near the spring line at the bottom of the escarpment.

clay

Water remains in the chalk

Quarrying causes a *Conflict* of land use

Granite, limestone and chalk are all quarried — which produces conflicts between the <u>quarrying companies</u>, <u>locals</u> and the <u>tourist industry</u>.

GOOD THINGS ABOUT QUARRIES	BAD THINGS ABOUT QUARRIES
Quarries provide building materials, cement and lime (which is used in fertilisers).	They're noisy, dusty eyesores which put people off coming to the area.
They provide employment at the quarry and associated businesses like road building, haulage, catering etc.	They increase the traffic.
When the quarrying has stopped they can be used as lakes for wildlife reserves and sporting stuff.	When the quarrying has stopped they're often used as landfill sites which can be bad for the environment.

Nowadays it is <u>very hard</u> to get permission to start or extend a quarry, especially in a tourist area.

Soils

Soils are the substances in which plants grow. They are made of both living and non-living material.

Vegetation, Climate, Rock Type and Soil Types are Linked

Areas with similar climates, vegetation and rock type tend to have similar soil types. Soils have five components —

1) Minerals (from rocks) in the form of silt, clay and sand.
2) Water from rain.
3) Air between lumps.
4) Organic matter like dead plant and animal remains and decomposed material.
5) Organisms like woodlice, bacteria and worms.

Soils have Four Main Characteristics

1) TEXTURE refers to particle size, e.g. sandy, clay, silt etc.
2) STRUCTURE means how the particles are arranged, e.g. crumbly, blocky.
3) COLOUR depends on its mineral and organic content, e.g. black means lots of organic matter; blue means lack of oxygen and waterlogging; red or brown means lots of oxygen and iron compounds.
4) ACIDITY refers to how acidic or alkaline the soil is. It's measured in pH on a scale from 1 to 14, with most soils between the range of 5 (acid) to 8 (alkaline).

A Profile shows the Layers of a Soil Type

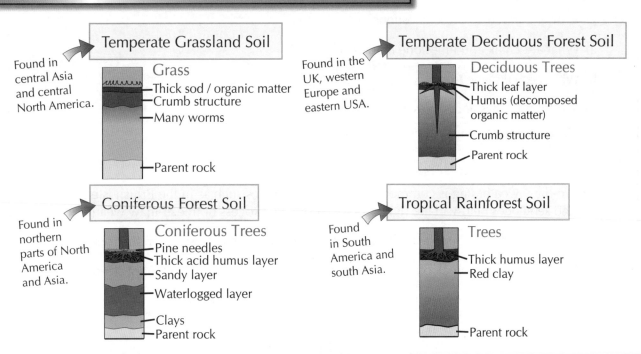

Found in central Asia and central North America.

Temperate Grassland Soil
Grass
— Thick sod / organic matter
— Crumb structure
— Many worms
— Parent rock

Found in the UK, western Europe and eastern USA.

Temperate Deciduous Forest Soil
Deciduous Trees
— Thick leaf layer
— Humus (decomposed organic matter)
— Crumb structure
— Parent rock

Found in northern parts of North America and Asia.

Coniferous Forest Soil
Coniferous Trees
— Pine needles
— Thick acid humus layer
— Sandy layer
— Waterlogged layer
— Clays
— Parent rock

Found in South America and south Asia.

Tropical Rainforest Soil
Trees
— Thick humus layer
— Red clay
— Parent rock

Some odd terms — but you, I know, will master them

This page is tough but you've got to know it. Read it through a couple of times first. Then scribble a list of soil components and characteristics.

Questions

OK, so that wasn't the most exciting section in the world. A load of pages on rocks, weathering and soil. But if you've learnt all of it then this little lot should be easy.

Warm-up Questions

1) What are the three main classes of rock?

2) What are sandstone, shales and clays made from?

3) What is biological weathering?

4) Name an example of a limestone landscape.

5) Describe two good things and two bad things about quarries.

6) Name the five components of soil.

Practice Questions

Take your time answering these questions, you need to get the basics right.

1) Write a definition for each of the types of rock below.

   a) Igneous

   b) Sedimentary

   c) Metamorphic

2) Give brief answers to these questions:

   a) What are chalk and limestone made from?

   b) What is coal made from?

   c) Sandstone, clays and shales are found in layers.
      What are these layers called?

3) Freeze-thaw weathering is common in temperate climates such as in the British Isles.
   Put the sentences below in the right order to show the process of freeze-thaw weathering.

   1. During the day, the ice melts, contracts and releases the pressure on the rock.

   2. Pieces of rock break off (frost shattering), producing scree at the foot of steep slopes.

   3. This alternating expansion and contraction weakens the rock.

   4. Water gets trapped in the cracks in rocks.

   5. When the temperature drops at night, the water freezes, expands and puts pressure on the rock sides.

Questions

4) Make three columns headed Granite, Limestone and Chalk.
    Copy the facts below under the correct headings (there are four for each).

    Very resistant to erosion.

    Can be used as a natural reservoir.

    Forms flat-topped moorlands with steep gorges.

    Impermeable, so water stays on the surface, creating marshes.

    Also known as karst scenery.

    Forms escarpments.

    Dartmoor has this type of rock.

    Quarried for lime, cement and building blocks.

    The Yorkshire Dales has this type of rock.

    Soil is infertile and unsuitable for farming.

    The South Downs has this type of rock.

    Soil is suitable for sheep farming and cereal crops.

5) Copy and label the diagram of a chalk escarpment below.

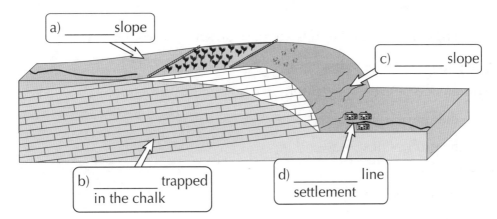

a) _____ slope

c) _____ slope

b) _____ trapped in the chalk

d) _____ line settlement

6) Join each word to its correct ending to make four sentences about soil characteristics.

    Texture   ...is black when there is a lot of organic matter.

    Structure   ...is measured in pH — usually 5 (acid) to 8 (alkaline).

    Colour   ...can be sandy, clay, silt, etc.

    Acidity   ...can be of crumbly or blocky particles.

Section Three — Summary Questions

There's a lot to get sorted in this section about rocks, weathering and soil. Quite a few tricky words and phrases packed in here — get these cracked and you'll be laughing. Have a go at the questions. If you get stuck or have problems then look back over the section until it's all clear.

1) Name the three types of rock.

2) What are igneous rocks formed from?

3) What is the difference between extrusive and intrusive rocks?

4) What are sedimentary rocks formed from?

5) How are metamorphic rocks formed?

6) What is weathering?

7) Describe the two types of physical weathering.

8) What happens to rock surfaces when they're heated?

9) Give two examples of biological weathering.

10) Describe how chemical weathering affects a limestone area.

11) a) Draw and label a diagram of a limestone landscape.

    b) Name an example of a limestone landscape.

12) Granite is impermeable. What does this mean?

13) What is the difference between erosion and weathering?

14) Is chalk porous or non-porous?

15) Give two good things and two bad things about quarries.

16) What are the five main components of a soil?

17) Describe the difference between the texture of a soil and its structure.

18) What affects the colour of soil?

19) Draw and label the profiles of soils found in:

    a) temperate grassland

    b) temperate deciduous forest

    c) coniferous forest

Climate Changes

Before you find out all about the weather and climate <u>today</u>,
you need to know a bit about how it's <u>changed</u> in the <u>past</u>.

Climate *is the* Average Weather Conditions *of a* Place

1) <u>Climate change</u> is any <u>major</u> change in the <u>weather</u> of a region over a long period of time. E.g. increasing average <u>temperature</u> or <u>rainfall</u>.

2) The climate <u>constantly changes</u>, it always has, and it always will.

3) For the last 2.5 million years, global temperature has shifted between <u>cold glacial</u> periods and <u>warmer interglacial periods</u>.

4) The <u>glacial</u> periods lasted about <u>100 000</u> years, and the <u>interglacial</u> periods lasted about <u>10 000</u> years.

5) We're in an <u>interglacial</u> period <u>now</u>.

Global Temperature *has been* Increasing

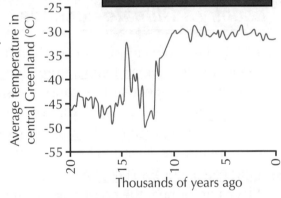

Temperature change in Greenland over the last 20 000 years

1) <u>20 000</u> years ago the Earth was cold. Around <u>12 000</u> years ago it started to warm up — this was the end of the last glacial period.

2) Over the last <u>10 000</u> years, the climate has mainly been <u>warm</u>.

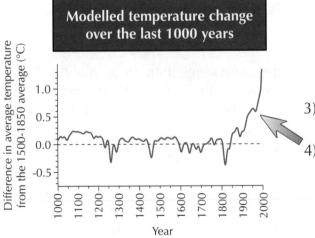

Modelled temperature change over the last 1000 years

3) Over the last <u>1000 years</u> the climate has been fairly <u>constant</u>.

4) Over the last century, temperatures across the globe have <u>increased rapidly</u>. This is called <u>global warming</u>.

5) The temperature <u>increase</u> over the last century has been very <u>fast</u>. Many scientists think that the <u>changes</u> in <u>climate</u> over the last century are a result of <u>human activities</u>.

Recording temperature change isn't hard graft with these graphs

A key point to remember about climate change is that the climate has always been changing. Global warming is just the large and rapid change we're experiencing now.

World Climate Zones

The world has several **Climatic Zones**

The world's climate zones are based on <u>maximum</u> and <u>minimum temperatures</u> and the <u>temperature range</u>, as well as <u>total</u> and <u>seasonal</u> distribution of <u>precipitation</u>.

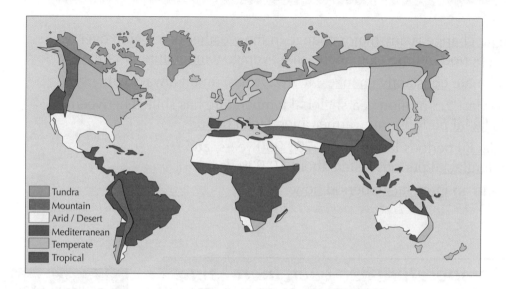

Tundra
Mountain
Arid / Desert
Mediterranean
Temperate
Tropical

A country's **Climate** depends on **Five Factors**

1) <u>LATITUDE</u> (how far north or south of the equator a place is):
Generally the <u>overall temperature decreases</u>, and <u>temperature range increases</u>, as you go <u>further</u> from the equator, because the sun's angle is <u>lower</u> nearer the poles.

2) <u>ALTITUDE</u> (height above sea-level):
Generally <u>temperatures decrease</u> where there is an <u>increase in height</u> above sea-level, and upland areas tend to be wetter as well.

3) <u>DISTANCE FROM THE SEA</u>:
Places on or near the <u>coast</u> have a <u>smaller temperature range</u> than those inland. This is because land heats up and cools down more quickly than the sea. Inland areas are drier, as wet winds from the sea have lost most of their moisture before they reach here.

4) <u>PREVAILING WINDS</u> (the usual direction of the wind in a place):
If these are <u>warm</u> (i.e. they've blown from a hot area) they'll <u>raise the temperature</u>. If they come from <u>colder areas</u> they'll <u>lower it</u>. If they come from the sea (onshore) or a wet area they'll bring <u>rain</u>. If they're offshore or blew over a <u>dry area</u> they'll be <u>dry</u>.

5) The world has <u>six major wind belts</u> and an area's <u>position</u> relative to these tells us its <u>precipitation</u> (rainfall) <u>characteristics</u>. These belts move north and south, with the overhead sun causing wet and dry seasons in some areas as the winds change direction during the year.

Keep checking the map as you learn this lot — it'll make more sense

This lot shouldn't be too hard to learn. These are the basic topics for this section — everything else will be a lot easier if you get this page clear right at the beginning.

World Climate Zones

Climate can be shown on a Graph

A climate graph consists of a line graph showing temperature, and a bar chart showing precipitation for each month of the year. The data used is usually the average for a period of years to eliminate unusual conditions. The shapes of the graphs can be used to identify different types of climate.

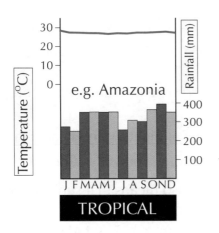

TROPICAL

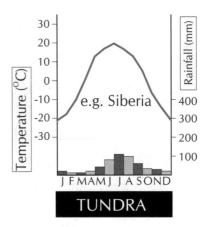

TUNDRA

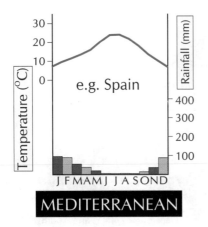

MEDITERRANEAN

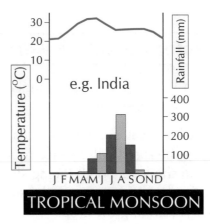

TROPICAL MONSOON

Remember — if a graph is for a place south of the Equator, they have opposite seasons to ours in the northern hemisphere — so July will be the coldest month.

There are clear patterns here, make sure you can spot them

Scribble a list of the five factors that create a country's climate, and jot down a quick paragraph to say how a climate graph works. Remember — it's all about getting the basic principles first.

Microclimates

Climate can Vary within a small area

A <u>microclimate</u> is where there are <u>local differences</u> in the climate.
This can be due to a variety of reasons linked to local environmental features.

Urban areas have a Microclimate different from rural areas

1) Urban areas have a <u>higher average temperature</u> than the surrounding countryside —
    up to 4°C at night and 1.6°C in the day. This is called the '<u>urban heat island effect</u>'.
    This is because:
    *   Buildings and roads act like <u>storage heaters</u>, absorbing the sun's heat during the
        day and letting it out at night.
    *   The air is full of <u>pollutants</u> which act as a blanket at night to stop heat getting out.
    *   Heat is <u>added</u> to the air from central heating, factories, power stations, etc.

2) The high level of <u>pollutant particles</u> in the urban air also means that <u>sunshine levels
    are low</u>, and there's more <u>cloud</u>, <u>rain</u> and <u>fog</u> than in rural areas.

3) Urban areas are either <u>very windy</u> because tall buildings cause a <u>wind tunnel effect</u>, or
    have <u>less wind</u> than nearby due to the air speed being <u>slowed</u> down by them (friction).

Other Factors affect local microclimates

1) <u>COLOUR OF SURFACE</u>: Dark surfaces absorb <u>more heat</u> than light ones, which
    <u>reflect heat</u> from the sun.

2) <u>ASPECT</u> (which way something faces): If a
    place <u>faces the sun</u> it will receive more heat
    than one in shadow. South-facing slopes in
    the northern hemisphere catch the sun and
    are usually used to grow crops.
    North-facing slopes are cooler and are used
    for grazing or are wooded. (It's the other
    way round in the southern hemisphere).

3) <u>WATER AREAS</u>: Lakesides are <u>more
    humid</u>, with more cloud and rain.
    They are <u>windy</u> due to less friction.

4) <u>SURFACE COVER</u>: Bare surfaces are
    <u>windier</u> than ones covered in vegetation.

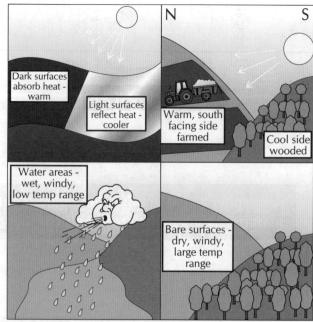

Microclimates are affected by lots of factors

When you think about <u>why</u> urban areas are warmer, cities don't seem quite as attractive.
Polluted air is an unpleasant side-effect of the concentration of people and industry in cities.

Types of Weather

Weather is the condition of the atmosphere at a certain time and place.

There are **Five** different **Elements** of **Weather**

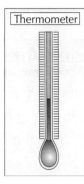
Thermometer

(1) TEMPERATURE

Temperature is how hot or cold the air is. It is measured using a thermometer. It is recorded in degrees Celsius (°C).

(2) AIR PRESSURE

Air pressure is the force the air exerts on an area due to its weight. Pressure is normally described as 'low' or 'high'. Low pressure is caused by warm air rising and high pressure is caused by cool air sinking. Looking at whether it's rising or falling means you can predict weather. Pressure is measured using a barometer which gives a reading in millibars (mb).

Barometer

(3) WIND

Wind is the movement of air. Air moves from areas of high pressure to areas of low pressure, so the wind blows towards the area of low pressure. Wind speed is measured with an anemometer. Wind direction is observed by using a wind vane. The arrow points to where the wind has come from.

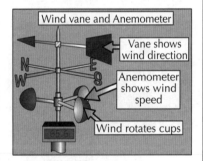
Wind vane and Anemometer
Vane shows wind direction
Anemometer shows wind speed
Wind rotates cups

(4) PRECIPITATION

Precipitation is the name for all water that falls from clouds. This includes rain, fog, hail, sleet and snow. Precipitation is measured using a rain gauge. It is recorded in millimetres (mm).

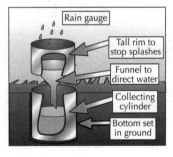
Rain gauge
Tall rim to stop splashes
Funnel to direct water
Collecting cylinder
Bottom set in ground

(5) CLOUDS

Clouds are water droplets suspended in the atmosphere. They're formed when water vapour condenses. You can't measure clouds using an instrument — you just have to observe them. The type of cloud and the amount of sky it covers is normally recorded.

Make sure you know the five elements and how to measure them

Don't get confused between weather and climate — weather is the condition of the atmosphere at a specific time and place and climate is the average weather conditions of a place.

Types of Weather

Precipitation is just the formal word for moisture that falls from clouds, e.g. rain, snow and hail. There are three main types of rainfall — relief, convectional and frontal.

Moist Air over Mountains gives Relief Rainfall

1) If warm, wet, onshore winds reach a mountain barrier they have to rise over it.
2) The air cools and its water vapour condenses. Clouds are formed and precipitation starts.
3) When the air has reached the summit the drier air starts to descend.
4) The air becomes warmer as it descends and any remaining clouds evaporate.
5) This drier area is known as a rain shadow.

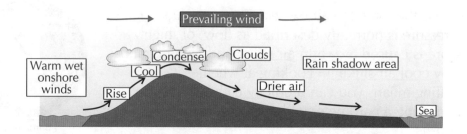

Convectional Rainfall — the sun heats the ground

Convectional rainfall occurs all year round in equatorial areas — and can occur in areas like the U.K. when the temperatures are high.

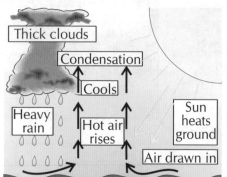

1) The sun heats the ground and warm air rises vertically.
2) As the air rises it cools, the water vapour condenses and thick storm clouds are formed.
3) This produces rainfall that is heavy and intense and is sometimes accompanied by thunder and lightning.

Frontal Rainfall occurs where Air Masses Meet

1) The boundary between two air masses of different temperatures is called a front.
2) When warm air masses and cold air masses meet, the warm air is forced upwards because it is less dense. The warm air cools and water vapour condenses causing frontal rain.
3) There are two types of front:
   - A cold front is where the cold air is pushing the warm air.
   - A warm front is where the warm air rises over the denser, cold air.

Cover up the page and sketch out the diagrams

The diagrams may look straightforward but you've got to make sure you know them inside out. We get all three types of rainfall in the UK — and don't we know it.

Weather Forecasting

Weather forecasting is predicting what the weather will be in the future.

We need to know what the Weather's going to be Like

It's really important to know what the weather forecast is because there are loads of things that are affected by the weather:

- Transport, e.g. ferries can't sail in high winds.
- Sport, e.g. tennis is cancelled when it's raining and skiing isn't very good with no snow.
- Energy production, e.g. wind turbines can't be used in very high winds.
- Tourism, e.g. outdoor events may be cancelled if rain is forecast.
- Farming, e.g. hay must be made in a period of dry weather.

Weather Forecasts are produced from lots of Data

All over the UK there are weather stations which collect weather data (see p.41). This can be used to draw maps or charts. Weather experts called meteorologists study these maps and charts — they compare the data with past situations to predict the future weather (hopefully).

Weather Maps show Lows and Highs

Lows are areas of low pressure (sometimes called depressions). They bring with them distinctive bad weather — rain and wind.

Highs are areas of high pressure (sometimes called anticyclones) and they are associated with good weather — blue skies and sunshine.
Lows and highs are both shown by a series of isobars in a roughly circular shape. Lows have isobar readings which decrease in value towards the centre — highs are the opposite.

Isobars are lines joining points of equal pressure.

Weather Maps Summarise the Weather

Meteorologists often produce weather maps like the ones in newspapers, which summarise what the weather's going to be like.

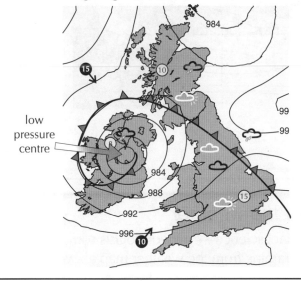

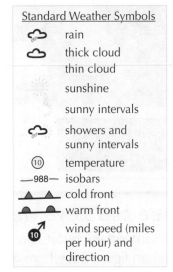

Standard Weather Symbols
- rain
- thick cloud
- thin cloud
- sunshine
- sunny intervals
- showers and sunny intervals
- temperature
- isobars
- cold front
- warm front
- wind speed (miles per hour) and direction

Weather Forecasting

Nowadays weather maps on TV are pretty accurate. That's because satellites can transmit images taken from a great height above the earth — giving a good view of the cloud formations below.

Satellite Images help us Understand the weather

1) Since the 1960s <u>satellite images</u> of clouds have been used to <u>predict weather</u>.

2) These are <u>transmitted</u> to us by satellites orbiting the earth and give us a good <u>overall view</u> of the world's weather situation.

3) On visible images, any <u>light surfaces</u> (like clouds) <u>reflect light</u> and appear <u>white</u> whilst <u>dark surfaces</u> (like the sea) appear <u>black</u>.

4) <u>Infra-red images</u> show the <u>temperature</u> of a surface — the <u>lighter</u> the colour, the <u>colder</u> the temperature is.

5) On images of the U.K. it's easy to see <u>lows</u> with circular patterns of white cloud.

Converting to Weather Maps

1) Images from satellites can be <u>converted</u> into weather maps.

2) The warm and cold fronts occur at the <u>edges</u> of the cloud formations.

3) The clouds usually circle around areas of <u>low pressure</u>.

4) The <u>isobars</u> follow the pattern of the clouds.

Here's an infra-red picture transmitted by a satellite orbiting the earth...

...and here's the weather map matching the satellite picture. It shows all the information given by the satellite in one diagram.

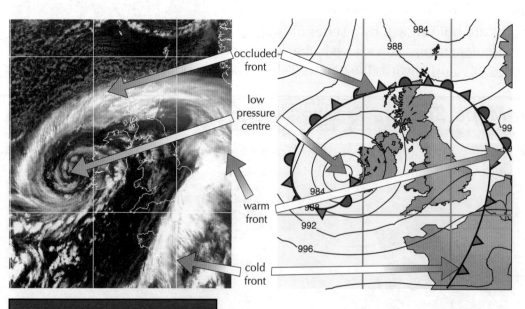

occluded front

low pressure centre

warm front

cold front

984
988
99
984
988
992
996

Occluded fronts occur when cold air goes underneath warm air.

Satellites give us a bird's eye view of the weather

Predicting the weather is important, but it's not an exact science — meteorologists sometimes get it wrong. See if you can figure out where it'd be raining from the weather map above.

The Hydrological Cycle

The Hydrological Cycle is the movement of a constant amount of water between the SEA, the LAND and the ATMOSPHERE. It's a continuous cycle with no starting or end point.

Condensation of water vapour forms **Clouds**

'Hydrological' is just a posh word for water.

Moist air blows towards land, rises and cools. Water vapour condenses forming clouds, and precipitation like rain, snow or hail falls on the ground below.

Rainwater *sinks into the* **Ground**

1) Water collects on plant leaves by interception, then drips off onto the soil.
2) It can then filter through the soil through spaces in the surface layers — infiltration.
3) The water can also move deeper into the unsaturated ground by percolation, until it reaches the water table (see p.46).

This water soon moves **Back** *to the* **Sea**

1) SURFACE RUN-OFF is when water flows overground to rivers, lakes or the sea.
2) CHANNEL FLOW is the flow of water in a stream, river or lake.
3) THROUGH FLOW is when infiltrated water moves through soil to a river.
4) GROUNDWATER FLOW is when percolated water moves below the water table to a river.

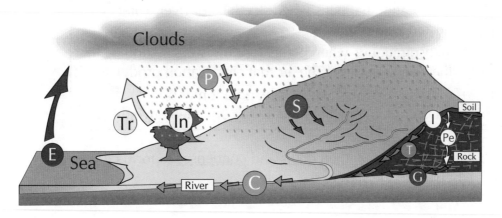

P Precipitation	**S** Surface Run-off	**I** Infiltration
In Interception	**C** Channel flow	**T** Through flow
Tr Transpiration	**E** Evaporation	**Pe** Percolation
		G Groundwater flow

The basics — make sure you know this stuff

Clouds form, it rains on the land, the water runs back into the sea through the ground and in rivers, it then evaporates, forming clouds — sounds like an average day in the UK.

The Hydrological Cycle

Some water is also **Stored** on the **Surface**

1) <u>CHANNEL STORAGE</u> happens in <u>rivers</u> and <u>lakes</u> and is vital for our <u>water supply</u>.

2) <u>GROUNDWATER STORAGE</u> occurs in <u>underground rocks</u> which are porous (full of tiny holes) — which means they <u>collect water</u>. The <u>water table</u> is the upper surface of <u>saturated rocks</u> in an area.

3) <u>SOIL MOISTURE STORAGE</u> is when water is stored in the <u>soil</u> and is used by <u>plants</u>.

4) <u>SHORT-TERM STORAGE</u> occurs after interception on <u>plant leaves</u>, <u>flowers</u>, etc.

Then the whole cycle **Starts Again**

<u>Water vapour</u> is produced by three things:

1) <u>Evaporation</u> happens when sea, lake or river water is heated by the <u>sun</u>.

2) <u>Transpiration</u> is when <u>plants</u> lose moisture — adding to the water vapour in the air that evaporation produces.

3) <u>Evapotranspiration</u> is both evaporation and transpiration together (and a very unimaginative title).

The water vapour produced <u>rises</u>, then <u>cools</u> and <u>condenses</u> to form <u>clouds</u>. This brings us right back to the start of the cycle.

Remember — <u>hydrological</u> is only a fancy way of talking about water

List the terms here until you've got them thoroughly stuck into your head. And next time you have a drink of water think about where it <u>came from</u>, and where it <u>goes to</u> next.

Questions

That section wasn't so bad... just a few clouds and some rain, nothing too hard.
Weather and climate are really important because they affect us all. Be careful not to get
the two terms confused.

Warm-up Questions

1) Name the five main factors that affect a country's climate.

2) What happens to temperature and rainfall as altitude increases?

3) Describe three ways in which the climate of an urban area can be different from that of the surrounding countryside.

4) What are satellite images? How might they help weather forecasters do their job?

5) How are clouds formed?

Practice Questions

Now that you're warmed-up have a bash at the longer practice questions.

1) Copy out the paragraph below using the correct words.

   Increasing average temperature is an example of **(flooding / climate change)**. The climate **(rarely / constantly)** changes. For the past **(2.5 million / 2.5 thousand)** years, global temperatures have shifted between **(cold / mild)** glacial periods and warmer interglacial periods. We're currently in **(an interglacial / a glacial)** period.

2) The map below shows the climate zones for part of the world, five of which are labelled. Match the climate zones from the list with their correct letters on the map.

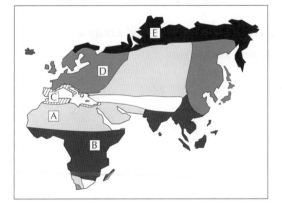

   Mediterranean
   Tropical
   Arid / Deserts
   Temperate
   Tundra

3) Copy and complete the sentences about climate below by choosing the correct word from each pair:

   a) Temperature usually **(increases / decreases)** as you go higher up mountains.

   b) There is usually **(more / less)** rainfall on high ground than on lower ground.

   c) Coastal areas have a **(smaller / larger)** temperature range than those further inland.

Questions

4) Look at this climate graph. Decide which climatic zone the country is located within and explain how you know.

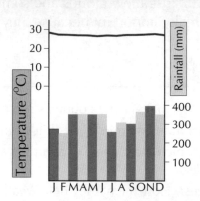

5) Copy the table and fill in the blanks.

Weather	Measured using	Recorded in
Temperature		degrees Celsius
	barometer	
Precipitation	rain gauge	
		coverage of sky

6) Look at the diagram of relief rainfall below.
Then match the words listed below to the correct letter on the diagram.

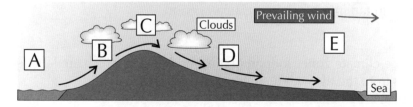

drier air   **warm, wet onshore winds**   **air rises and cools**
rain shadow area   **water vapour condenses**

7) State which of the sentences below are true and which are false. Then write a correction for the false statements.

a) In hot equatorial areas, convectional rainfall occurs all year round.

b) Heated air spreads out on the Earth's surface and causes rain.

c) A cold front is where the warm air is pushing the cold air.

d) Convectional rain occurs in the UK when temperatures are high.

e) Thermal up-currents cause low air pressure.

8) What weather system would be ideal for a sports day — high pressure or low pressure? Explain your answer.

9) The lines showing air pressure on a map are usually a roughly circular shape. How can you tell the difference between a high and a low pressure system?

Section Four — Summary Questions

The key to this section is getting the diagrams and technical terms clear in your head. Remember, everything in this section is here because it's really important for you to know it — you just have to get it learned. Don't forget to practise these questions over and over again until you can answer them easily. Then you can move on.

1) What is climate change?

2) Briefly describe the pattern of climate change that's been happening over the last 2.5 million years.

3) How does the latitude of a place affect its climate?

4) Describe how the distance between a place and the sea affects climate.

5) What are prevailing winds? How do they influence climate?

6) Name two other factors that affect climate.

7) What would a climate graph of a Mediterranean climate look like? Draw an example.

8) Why is it warmer in urban areas than in surrounding rural areas?

9) Write briefly how the following factors can affect local microclimates:
   a) the colour and cover of the surface; b) an area of water; c) the aspect.

10) What instruments are used to measure the following:
    a) temperature; b) rainfall; c) pressure?

11) How are wind speed and wind direction measured?

12) What is meant by the term precipitation?

13) With the aid of a labelled diagram explain relief rainfall.

14) Where in the world is convectional rainfall found? How does it form? Draw and label a diagram to help you explain your answer.

15) What is frontal rainfall linked with?

16) Name five things that can be affected by the weather.

17) What is the proper name for a weather expert?

18) Draw the weather map symbol for a cold front.

19) What kind of weather do you get in areas of low pressure?

20) What are areas of high pressure also known as?

21) What are isobars? What do they show?

22) Draw simple sketch diagrams of the isobar pattern for a low and a high.

23) What do lows look like on satellite images?

24) How are clouds formed?

25) Draw a diagram of the hydrological cycle and label it.

26) What are the four ways that water moves back to the sea?

27) What is transpiration?

Drainage Basins

Here are a few pages about rivers, so let's just go with the flow and read all about them.

A *Drainage Basin* is a land area drained by a river

1) A drainage basin is the land area from which a river and its tributaries collect the rainwater passing through the soil and rock.

2) Tributaries are the smaller branches of the river, that join the main channel.

3) A watershed is high ground separating two neighbouring drainage basins. On one side of it, the water drains in one direction and on the other side it drains the opposite way.

4) The start of a river is called the source.

5) Some basins are very large, e.g. the Amazon drainage basin covers most of Brazil.

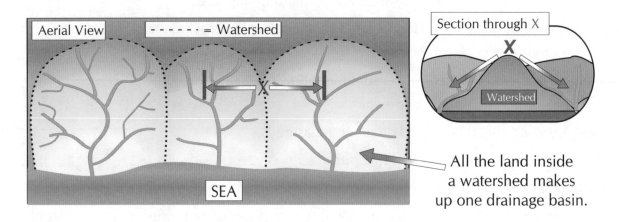

All the land inside a watershed makes up one drainage basin.

A drainage basin works as a *System*

1) Water enters the drainage basin as precipitation (rain, snow and hail). It moves from the high ground to the sea both above ground (in rivers) and below ground. Sometimes the water is stored in soil and vegetation temporarily. It eventually drains into a river and flows into the sea (river run-off).

2) The time between rainfall and the water entering the sea varies with the basin's characteristics — e.g. shape and size, rock type and vegetation.

3) Energy is put into the system by the steepness of the hills / valley and the force of gravity.

4) Water moves rock and soil material through the drainage basin system. It's picked up when the water energy is high and deposited when the energy is low.

Drainage basins work as a continual, on-going system

Copy out the diagram of the drainage basin system above and learn it. But also try to think about where the water comes from, where it goes and how it gets there.

Drainage Basins

A **River Basin** has several important features

1. The <u>source</u> is where a river <u>starts</u>, usually in an upland area.

2. A <u>tributary</u> is a <u>stream</u> that joins the main river.

3. A <u>confluence</u> is the point where two rivers join.

4. The <u>mouth</u> is where the river flows into the sea.

5. An <u>estuary</u> is where the mouth is <u>low enough</u> to let the <u>sea enter</u> at high tide — <u>deposition</u> in estuaries forms mud and sand banks which the river flows between.

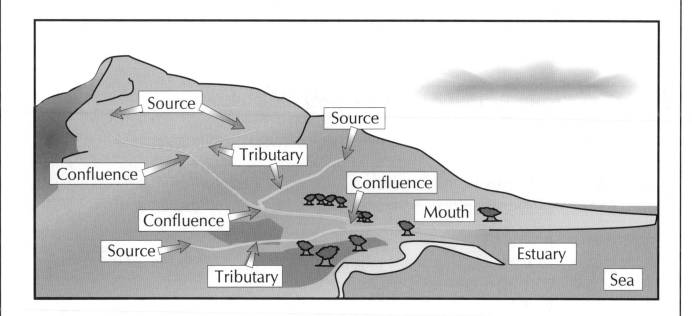

Cover the page, and list the features of river basins in order

Not too much to deal with here. You just need to make sure that you know the terms and remember that it's a <u>system</u> — the order that the stages come in is really important.

Rivers and Valleys

Rivers change as they make their way to the sea. This affects the characteristics of the valleys they flow through.

River Characteristics Change *as you move towards the sea*

1) A <u>river</u> flows from an <u>upland source</u> to the <u>mouth</u>, where it enters the sea.

2) The river channel <u>widens</u> as it follows its course to the sea.

3) The <u>discharge</u> (the amount of water that flows in a river per second) increases as <u>other</u> streams and rivers <u>join it</u>.

4) A <u>river's energy</u> is linked to its <u>velocity</u> — the speed of flow in one direction. <u>High velocity</u> means <u>high energy</u> — e.g. during floods or when the river's gradient is steep.

5) Rivers with <u>lots of energy</u> wear away the <u>channel bed</u> and <u>banks</u> producing the <u>load</u> — sand and stones.

6) When a river has <u>little energy</u>, the load is <u>deposited</u> on the <u>bed</u> and <u>banks</u>.

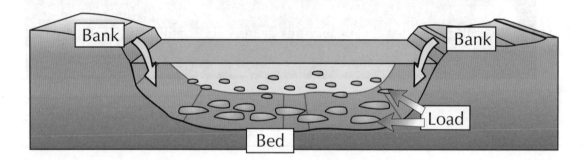

A valley Cross Profile *has Three Stages*

1) <u>UPPER</u>: near to the river's source the valley has a <u>narrow floor</u> and <u>steep sides</u> — it's the shape of the letter 'V'.

2) <u>MIDDLE</u>: lower down the river, the <u>floor</u> is <u>wider</u> and the <u>sides</u> are more <u>gently sloping</u>.

3) <u>LOWER</u>: when the river is near to the sea it has a <u>wide floor</u> and <u>gentle sides</u>.

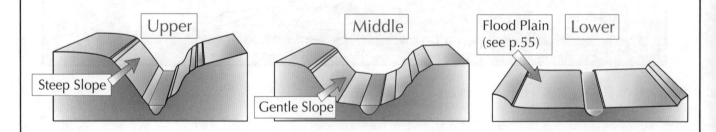

The shape of a valley changes as it reaches the sea

Learn the three stages in the cross profile of a valley. A good way to learn this page is to see if you can draw the diagrams without looking.

Rivers and Valleys

A river's **Long Profile** varies as it moves downstream

1) In the <u>upper</u> stage, the river's gradient is quite <u>steep</u>.
2) In the <u>middle</u> stage it's <u>more gentle</u>.
3) In the <u>lower</u> stage it's <u>very gentle</u> and almost <u>flat</u>.

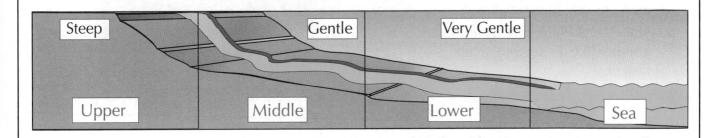

Erosion is when the river *Wears* land *Away*

Rivers erode in four main ways, called <u>erosion processes</u>:

1) <u>Abrasion</u> is when <u>large pieces</u> of load material (stones and sand carried by the river) <u>wear away</u> the <u>riverbed</u> and <u>banks</u> — e.g. in floods. If material collects in a dip, it swirls round forming a <u>pothole</u>.

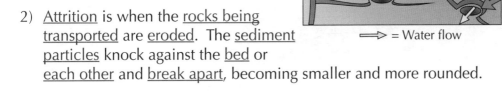

Swirling water and pebbles fall into a little hole and turn it into a bigger hole called a pothole.

⟹ = Water flow

2) <u>Attrition</u> is when the <u>rocks being transported</u> are <u>eroded</u>. The <u>sediment particles</u> knock against the <u>bed</u> or <u>each other</u> and <u>break apart</u>, becoming smaller and more rounded.

3) <u>Hydraulic action</u> is when the <u>force of the water</u> wears away at <u>softer rocks</u> such as clay. It can also <u>weaken rocks</u> along bedding planes and joints (see p.30).

4) <u>Corrosion</u> is when chalk and limestone <u>dissolve</u> in water.

Erosion — when the river slowly wears away the earth surrounding it

Learn the <u>four kinds</u> of <u>erosion</u> listed above by heart. Shut the book and scribble them down. You need to get your head round them because some of them pop up in later topics.

River Features of the Upper Stage

Interlocking Spurs are caused by Erosion

1) In its <u>upper stage</u> the river <u>erodes</u> <u>vertically</u> (downwards) rather than <u>laterally</u> (sideways).

2) <u>Interlocking spurs</u> are <u>ridges</u> produced when a river in the upper stage <u>twists</u> and <u>turns</u> round obstacles of <u>hard rock</u> along its downward pathway.

3) These ridges <u>interlock</u> with one another like the teeth of a zip fastener.

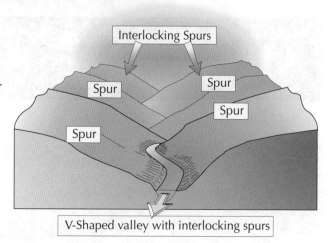

V-Shaped valley with interlocking spurs

Waterfalls are found at Steep parts of the river bed

1) A layer of hard rock <u>won't</u> erode very easily so when the river reaches it, any softer rocks on the <u>downstream side</u> (after the hard rock) are <u>eroded</u> more <u>quickly</u> forming a <u>waterfall</u>.

2) At the <u>foot</u> of the waterfall the water <u>wears away</u> the softer rock to form a <u>plunge pool</u> (a deep pool).

3) <u>Undercutting</u> causes rocks to collapse, so the waterfall's position retreats upstream and a <u>gorge</u> forms.

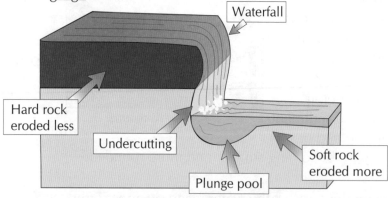

Waterfall

Hard rock eroded less

Undercutting

Plunge pool

Soft rock eroded more

Rapids are a series of little waterfalls

They're found where there are <u>alternative bands</u> of <u>hard</u> and <u>soft rock</u>. The soft rock is eroded more quickly than the hard rock and an uneven river bed is formed.

Rapids

Waterfalls and spurs — time for a rapid recap

Remember — <u>interlocking spurs</u>, <u>waterfalls</u> and <u>rapids</u> are the key features of a river in the <u>upper stage</u>. Try scribbling down a list of the ways in which each feature is <u>formed</u>.

River Features of the Middle and Lower Stages

The *Middle* and *Lower* stages have *Meanders*

1) The river now has a <u>large discharge</u> (large volume of water in it per second), a <u>gentle gradient</u> and is eroding <u>laterally</u> (sideways).

2) It develops a more winding pathway with <u>large bends</u> — these bends are called <u>MEANDERS</u>.

3) The river twists like a snake from side to side.

4) The <u>current is fastest</u> on the <u>outside</u> of the meander curve and the river channel is <u>deeper</u> there. On the <u>inside</u> it's <u>shallow</u> and the <u>current</u> is <u>slower</u>.

5) <u>River cliffs</u> are found on the meander's <u>outer edge</u> where the fast flow causes more erosion.

6) <u>Point bars</u> are on the <u>inner edge</u> where sandy material is <u>deposited</u> by the <u>slower-moving river</u>.

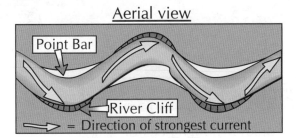

Aerial view

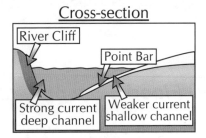

Cross-section

Ox-bow lakes are formed from wide meander loops

1) <u>Meander loops</u> can become so wavy that the river's easiest path is <u>straight across</u>, so it <u>breaks through</u> the narrow <u>neck of land</u> in between. This usually happens when the river is in flood.

2) The <u>outer part</u> of the loop is left <u>isolated</u> from the river. This loop is called an <u>Ox-Bow lake</u>.

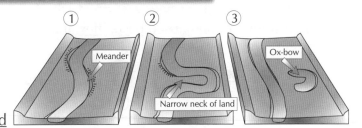

The *Lower Stage* has several *Important Features*

The river now has its greatest discharge and velocity — it has a really big cross-sectional area.

1) The <u>FLOOD PLAIN</u> is the <u>wide valley floor</u> which the river regularly <u>floods</u>. When it floods material carried by the river is deposited on the land. This material is often fertile making it good for <u>farming</u>.

2) <u>ESTUARIES</u> are <u>funnel-shaped river mouths</u>. Most are found where an existing river has had its lower reaches flooded after changes in <u>sea level</u>.

3) <u>DELTAS</u> form when a river deposits its load <u>too fast</u> for the sea to remove it — because the sea is <u>tideless</u>, e.g. the Nile (Mediterranean), or the <u>load</u> is <u>too big</u>, e.g. the Ganges (Bay of Bengal).

Meandering rivers are <u>bendy</u> rivers — learn all about them <u>now</u>

Not too problematic. Careful with this stuff. It might not be too hard, but make sure you're very comfortable with it.

Flooding

Rivers are vital for lots of human activities, but they can be a major hazard as well. Floods are never good news, but the effects are generally <u>worse</u> in less economically developed countries (<u>LEDCs</u>). It's not all peaches and cream in more economically developed countries (<u>MEDCs</u>) though, as the first example shows.

Floods can cause **Extensive Damage**

Floods can damage more things than you'd think — it's not always just farmland that's affected.

Buildings	Farmland	Vehicles	Transport	Power	People

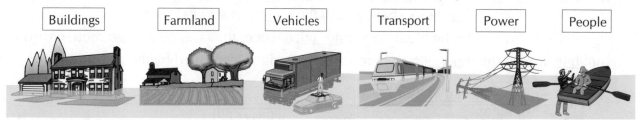

An **MEDC Flood Example** — Lynmouth, Devon 1952

1) There was <u>no early warning system</u> in spite of known <u>high peak discharges</u>:

 1.75cm rain per hour!

Rapid run-off

Saturated ground

 High water table

Rapid run-off (see p.50)
Short lag time (rain and flood water reached the rivers very quickly)

2) The resulting flood caused <u>casualties</u> and <u>damage</u>:

34 Dead

1000 Homeless

90 Buildings destroyed

150 Cars/boats lost

In an **LEDC** things can be even worse

1) Some <u>LEDCs</u> use river flooding to cover farmland with <u>fertile alluvium</u> and also to provide water for <u>irrigation channels</u> — e.g. the Ganges Valley and delta in Bangladesh.

2) <u>Severe floods</u> can destroy food supplies, homes, etc. <u>Emergency services</u> and <u>money</u> are <u>limited</u> in LEDCs, making recovery <u>more difficult</u>.

3) In 2004 <u>Bangladesh</u> experienced serious flooding. The floods <u>cost</u> the economy 2.2 billion US dollars and over 700 people were <u>killed</u>.

4) Floods are often completely <u>unexpected</u>. They usually happen in <u>flatter</u>, <u>lower-lying</u> old valleys which are often <u>built up</u> and <u>heavily populated</u>.

5) Flood disasters are worse in LEDCs because their flood <u>preparation</u>, <u>defence</u> and <u>recovery</u> are not as good as they are in MEDCs.

Flooding is a big problem in MEDCs and LEDCs alike

Both face the problem that a large percentage of settlements have been built around waterways. However, MEDCs often cope with flooding better because they have better flood management.

Flooding

When you think of flood control, it's probably the hard engineering bit you think of. Hard engineering involves building structures to control the river system — the big things, like dams. There's also soft engineering where natural drainage basin processes are used to reduce flooding.

Dams can Control Discharge for a whole valley

1) Dams and reservoirs in the upper parts of a drainage basin are very effective for controlling the discharge lower down the valley — where the flood threat is greatest. They can also be used to generate hydroelectric power and the reservoir can be used recreationally, e.g. sailing.

2) The disadvantages of schemes like this is that they are expensive to build, beautiful countryside can be spoiled by ugly buildings and good farmland can be destroyed when the upper valley floors are flooded.

You can change the River's Shape to Control Flooding

1) Increasing the capacity of the river channel means it can hold more water in a flood.

2) Culverts straighten and line the river channel to increase the speed of the river and remove excess water more quickly down the channel to the sea. To keep culverts working they have to be dredged to remove deposited material and stop the channel size decreasing. This increases the channel speed and can cause increased flooding and erosion downstream.

3) Building branching channels off the main river can remove the excess water. The excess water can be diverted around towns, moved to another drainage basin or stored.

   There are two disadvantages that apply to all the hard engineering options:
   1) The engineering often looks ugly and affects the natural river ecosystems.
   2) If the structure breaks there could be a very BIG, very SUDDEN disaster.
   To avoid these problems water authorities are moving to more sustainable flood controls, using 'soft engineering' such as changing land use.

Changing Land Use can help Reduce flooding

One of the easiest 'soft engineering' ways of avoiding flood problems is not to build houses where it floods. But lots of people already live in flood zones, so different strategies are needed.

1) Afforestation (planting trees) on bare slopes in the upper reaches reduces run-off as trees intercept (trap) the rain.

2) Leaving land up-river for grazing animals gives a continuous plant cover, reducing run-off water which the plants intercept. It's better than growing crops, where the soil is bare during the non-growing season.

3) Man-made surfaces, such as concrete, allow rapid run-off. Plants and grass areas can be used instead to reduce flooding in urban areas.

4) Soft engineering is used a lot in MEDCs where there's more money available to invest in flood prediction, prevention and control. In LEDCs hard engineering is the most common way of reducing flooding.

Questions

Here's some nice easy warm-up questions about rivers to get your brain fully working.

Warm-up Questions

1) Describe what these terms mean: Drainage basin; Watershed.
2) What do the following terms mean when referring to rivers?
   Load, discharge, bed, velocity, banks, channel.
3) What are interlocking spurs? At what stage of a river are they found?
4) How do rapids form?
5) Give an example of an LEDC where flooding is a problem and explain why floods in LEDCs often cause bigger problems than floods in MEDCs.

Practice Questions

Once you're confident that you know the basics really well have a go at these questions.

1) Give a brief description of each of the erosion processes named below.
   a) Attrition.
   b) Abrasion.
   c) Corrosion.
   d) Hydraulic action.

2) Use the diagrams below to write a short paragraph about what happens when a waterfall is formed.

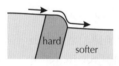
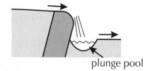
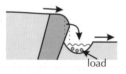

3) Look at the diagram which shows a cross-section of a river meander. Then copy the table and fit the words from below in the right place.

fast   slow   shallow   deep   cliff   beach (point bar)   deposition   erosion

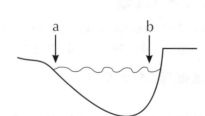

	a	b
speed		
depth		
process		
landform		

4) Long-term flood protection, such as dams and reservoirs, brings both advantages and disadvantages. Draw a table with two columns and list their good and bad points (at least three of each).

5) Describe in one sentence how soft engineering is different from hard engineering.

The Power of the Sea

Waves are <u>energy movements</u> through <u>water</u> caused by the <u>wind</u>
— they're the main way in which the sea erodes, transports and deposits material.

Wave *Energy* and *Movement*

The <u>energy of a wave</u> is determined by its <u>height</u> (distance between its
trough and crest) and <u>length</u> (distance between two crests).

1) Wave height and length <u>vary</u> according to the <u>speed</u> and
   <u>length of time</u> a wave has been moving, and the <u>fetch</u> —
   the distance of open sea over which the wind has blown.

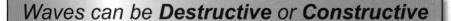

2) Near the coast, waves <u>slow down</u> in the shallow water, causing them to 'break', becoming
   unstable. Seawater moving up the beach is <u>swash</u>, and moving back to the sea is <u>backwash</u>.

Waves can be *Destructive* or *Constructive*

1) <u>DESTRUCTIVE WAVES</u> operate in storm conditions and are
   tall (can be several metres high). The <u>backwash</u> is strong and
   there is <u>a lot of erosion</u>.

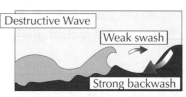

2) <u>CONSTRUCTIVE WAVES</u> operate in calm weather and are
   less tall (usually less than 1m). The <u>swash</u> is strong and
   erosion is <u>limited</u>. They're involved with the <u>transport</u> and
   <u>deposition</u> of material creating landforms (see p 61).

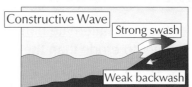

The sea *Erodes* the coast in *Five Ways*

1) <u>HYDRAULIC ACTION</u> — lots of sea water crashes against the land, and air and water are
   trapped and <u>compressed</u> in rock surface cracks. When the sea moves away again the air
   <u>expands</u> explosively weakening the rocks, enlarging the cracks and <u>breaking</u> pieces off.

2) <u>CORRASION</u> (or <u>ABRASION</u>) is very effective and is caused by broken rock fragments
   <u>battering</u> the land, cliffs, etc. and <u>breaking off</u> other pieces of rock.

3) <u>ATTRITION</u> occurs when rock fragments <u>grind</u> each other down into smaller and smoother
   pebbles, shingle, and finally sand, which is later <u>deposited</u> as beaches, etc.

4) <u>CORROSION</u> involves <u>chemical action</u> of sea on rock. Weak acids and salts in seawater can
   dissolve some rock types, e.g. limestone.

5) <u>WAVE POUNDING</u> — the '<u>battering ram</u>' action of the <u>weight</u> of the pounding waves.

Waves can *Move Material* along the coast

1) <u>Longshore drift</u> happens when waves break at an <u>oblique angle</u> to the shore (not right angles)
   due to the prevailing wind.

2) This means that each wave pushes material <u>along</u> the beach a bit more.

3) Features can be formed by this process (see p 61).

Be sure of this lot before looking at the rest of the section

The energy and movement of waves explains why coasts form as they do. You should be able to
describe the different ways that the sea erodes the coast and what longshore drift is.

Coastal Landforms from Erosion

Wave erosion forms many coastal features over long periods of time.

Rock erosion forms **Cliffs**

1) Waves erode rocks along the shoreline by hydraulic action, corrosion, corrasion and pounding.

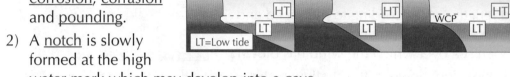

2) A notch is slowly formed at the high water mark which may develop into a cave.

3) Rock above the notch becomes unstable with nothing to support it, and it collapses.

4) The coastline can retreat over many years as this process continues to form a wave cut platform e.g. Robin Hood's Bay (Yorkshire) with cliffs behind.

5) The actual size and angle of the cliff will depend on the local rock and its hardness.

Eroded hard and soft rocks form **Headlands**

1) If there are alternate bands of hard and softer rock in the coastline, the harder rocks take longer to erode than the softer rocks — because the sea has less effect.

2) The hard rock will be left jutting out forming one or more headlands — usually with cliffs.

3) The softer rock will be eroded to form bays — a beach often forms.

4) Again the local geology will affect the actual shape and size of the features formed.

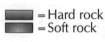
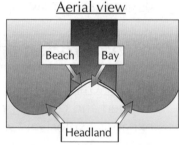

= Hard rock
= Soft rock

Caves, **Arches** and **Stacks** can also be formed

1) A crack or rock weakness in a headland can be eroded — wave energy is usually strong there because the headland juts out. This forms one or more caves, e.g. Fingal's Cave, Staffa.

2) Occasionally the pressure of air, compressed in the caves by the waves, weakens the roof along a major joint and the rock collapses to form a blow hole. Further erosion enlarges the cave and it breaks through the headland forming an arch, e.g. Durdle Door, Dorset.

3) The roof of this arch is often unstable and eventually collapses leaving a stack or series of stacks, e.g. The Needles off the Isle of Wight.

4) Areas with a limestone or chalk geology are prone to this kind of erosion.

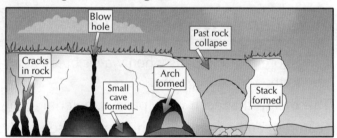

Soft rock erodes faster than hard rock

Make sure you learn the names of the main features of sea erosion and the way each feature is formed. Don't forget that local geology affects the size and shape of the feature formed.

Coastal Landforms from Deposition

Beaches *are formed by deposition*

Beaches are found on coastlines where eroded material in the sea has been deposited — e.g. in bays between headlands (see last page). They vary in size, from tiny Cornish inlets to vast stretches like Blackpool. Beach fragment size depends on local rock type and wave energy — e.g. fine sand at Blackpool, or pebbles at Hastings.

Storm beaches are ridges of boulders at the landward side of beaches caused by heavy seas piling up material at the high-tide mark.

Spits *are long beaches formed by longshore drift*

1) Spits are sand or pebble beaches sticking out to sea, but joined to the land at one end — they tend to be formed by the process of longshore drift (see p 59).

2) Spits tend to be formed:
   - across river mouths
   - where the coast suddenly changes direction
   - where tides meet calmer waters of a bay or inlet.

3) Waves can't reach the sea areas behind the spit, so they're often mud flats and salt marshes.

4) Examples are across the mouth of the River Exe in Devon.

There are also **Tombolos** and **Barrier Beaches**

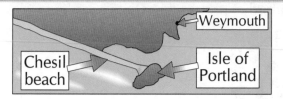

TOMBOLOS are found where an island is joined to the mainland by a ridge of deposited material, e.g. Chesil Beach on the South Coast, it's 18km long and it joins the Isle of Portland to the mainland.

BARRIER BEACHES are found where a spit extends right across a shallow bay, e.g. Slapton Sands, Devon — the water behind it is left as a lagoon, which may slowly become a marsh.

 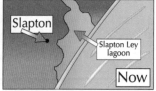

Beaches — formed from deposition

There are a few terms to get the hang of here. It's really important that you don't get any of this stuff confused. Don't skim over it. Remember, spits are just long beaches.

The Coast and People

Erosion, flooding and coastal land use cause a lot of conflict.

Coastal Protection is a priority

1) Coastal areas need to be <u>managed</u> carefully, either by national bodies such as the National Parks Authorities and the National Trust, or by local authorities.

> **Many coastlines are beautiful which is why lots of people visit them — but they're fragile and can be damaged by people trampling over them. Some are natural conservation areas with rare habitats which are easily destroyed.**

2) <u>Access</u> is possible with <u>limited disruption</u> and <u>damage</u> — e.g. authorised car parks and picnic sites, well-marked footpaths and information leaflets about erosion.

3) Footpaths can be <u>reinforced</u> and the areas at risk <u>fenced off</u> from the public.

Coastal Protection causes Many Conflicts

1) Residents want to <u>preserve</u> their homes and livelihoods.

2) Tourists want <u>access</u> to the coastal areas without restriction.

3) Conservationists want to <u>preserve local habitats</u> and <u>protect</u> wildlife.

4) The government has to consider the effect of an action in one place on other places nearby, and also to use public money in the <u>best</u> possible way, benefiting the most people.

5) Local authorities have to <u>look after</u> the <u>interests</u> of as many local people as possible in the most economical and satisfactory way.

6) Coastal protection is very expensive — we can't afford to protect the whole coastline.

Defending against sea damage is not a clear cut issue

There are several groups of people to consider when it comes to protecting the coast. Looking after the coastline often involves finding a balance between the interests of local people, conservationists, tourists and the government.

Flood and Erosion Control

There are <u>two</u> different approaches to <u>defend</u> against coastal erosion and flooding — <u>hard</u> and <u>soft</u> engineering. This page is about hard engineering methods.

There are **Five** main **Hard Engineering** defences

1) <u>GROYNES</u> are wooden structures placed at right angles to the coast where longshore drift occurs. They <u>reduce</u> movement of material along the coast, and <u>hold</u> the beach in place — <u>protecting</u> the shore from further erosion. A beach will naturally <u>protect</u> low areas from <u>flooding</u>.

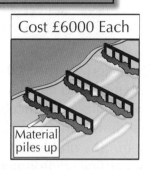

Cost £6000 Each

Material piles up

Cost £2000 per metre

sea wall   sea

2) <u>SEA WALLS</u> reduce erosion and protect against flooding in lowland areas. The problem is that they <u>deflect</u> (not absorb) the waves. This means the protective beach gets washed away. The waves also <u>erode</u> the wall itself which can collapse.

3) <u>REVETMENTS</u> (slatted barriers) are built where a sea wall is <u>too expensive</u>, e.g. out of towns. They <u>break</u> the wave force, trapping beach material behind them and <u>protecting</u> the cliff base — they're <u>more effective</u> than sea walls but look ugly and <u>don't</u> give full protection.

4) <u>GABIONS</u> are steel mesh cages containing boulders, built onto the cliff face or along a beach. The rocks <u>absorb</u> some of the wave energy and <u>cut down</u> erosion — they're cheap but ugly.

5) <u>ARMOUR BLOCKS</u> are large boulders piled on beaches where erosion is likely. They're cheap but ugly and they can be <u>moved by strong waves</u>.

> These <u>hard engineering</u> style sea defences are <u>not sustainable</u> in the long term. They are extremely <u>expensive</u>, <u>ugly</u>, need <u>constant</u> maintenance and often cause <u>problems</u> further down the coast.

None of these methods are perfect, but they have their merits

There are several factors you need to consider when choosing the best method of protecting the coast. You need to know this lot well, so you can compare hard engineering with soft engineering.

Flood and Erosion Control

A more *Sustainable* approach — *Soft Engineering*

The easiest soft engineering option is to leave the sea to do what it wants. The problem is that without control the sea would destroy a lot of land by floods and erosion. Soft engineering approaches try to fit in with natural coastal processes and protect habitats.

1) BEACH NOURISHMENT — This is the term for adding more mud or sand to the beach. The beach is an excellent natural flood defence so by replacing all the sediment that's eroded, you avoid a big flood problem. The problem is how to get the sediment without causing environmental damage somewhere else. It's also pretty expensive and needs to be done again and again.

2) SHORELINE VEGETATION — Planting things like marshbeds on the shoreline binds the beach sediment together, slowing erosion. This also encourages shoreline habitats to develop.

3) DUNE STABILISATION — Dunes are an excellent defence against storm floods. Sediment is added and erosion is reduced by footpath control and marram grass planting. This supports the dune ecosystem.

4) MANAGED RETREAT — Instead of continually pumping money into fighting a losing battle, managed retreat is about slowing coastal erosion but not trying to stop it. Eventually buildings will have to be moved or lost to the sea, but this can often be cheaper than investing in constant coastal control.

5) SET BACKS — This means building houses set back from the coast's edge.

It's quite a list, but make sure you learn it

Protecting the coastline is a good example of how people can help preserve the environment so that everyone can enjoy it without causing lots of damage. Jot down a paragraph on how coastlines can be protected — include both types of engineering and why they are good or bad.

The Work of Ice

During cold glacial periods, glaciers produced the landscape which we can see across much of the British Isles.

Many landscapes were shaped by Ice

Extent of glaciation over Britain

1) At various stages in Britain's geological history the climate got <u>colder</u>.

2) These <u>glacial periods</u> (see p. 37) were periods of intense <u>glacial activity</u>.

3) The last one started around 100,000 years ago and ended around 12,000 years ago.

4) During that time the <u>southern</u> and <u>eastern</u> parts of the British Isles had a climate like the one in <u>modern Tundra areas</u> (see p. 8), such as the regions in the far north around the Arctic Circle.

5) <u>All</u> of <u>Scotland</u> and the <u>north of England</u> were covered by an area of ice. Glaciers ('rivers' of ice which form in cold areas) formed and moved down valleys with great <u>erosive power</u>, like giant bulldozers, carving <u>new features</u>.

Three Ice Actions changed the landscape

1) <u>FREEZE-THAW ACTION</u>:
(see p 29) is a type of <u>weathering</u> where water settles in cracks in the rock surface, freezes and <u>expands</u>, pressurising surrounding rock. Then it thaws and <u>contracts</u>, releasing the pressure. Repeating the process <u>loosens</u> the surface and provides rock fragments for abrasion.

2) <u>ABRASION</u>:
is a process where rock fragments in the ice <u>grind</u> against the rock over which the ice is moving — like rough sandpaper — <u>wearing away</u> the land.

3) <u>PLUCKING</u> (QUARRYING):
occurs when meltwater at the base of a glacier <u>freezes</u> on the rock surface. As the glacier moves forward it <u>extracts</u> pieces from the rock surface.

Glaciers can move solid loads — the load is either frozen in the glacier, carried on its surface, or pushed in front of it. The load is deposited when the ice melts at the end of a glacial period.

(Remember that the load is anything carried by a river, glacier or sea.)

You need to know about the processes that changed the landscape

You need to know a bit about the history of glacial activity to understand how these ice actions came to shape the landscape. There are a few words to remember here, but nothing too tricky.

The Work of Ice

Glaciers are **Similar** to rivers

(1) Both start in <u>highland areas</u> — glaciers start when the climate is so cold that winter snow and ice don't melt in summer. Ice builds up in mountain-top hollows — on the colder, north-facing slopes.

(2) They both flow <u>downhill</u>, although a glacier is slower — it only moves 3 to 300 metres per year.

(3) A river flows into the <u>sea</u>, while a glacier ends in a <u>snout</u>, or in the <u>sea</u>.

(4) Both have distinctive <u>cross profiles</u> and <u>long profiles</u>.

(5) In both cases, <u>upland areas</u> have erosion features and <u>lowlands</u> have depositional features.

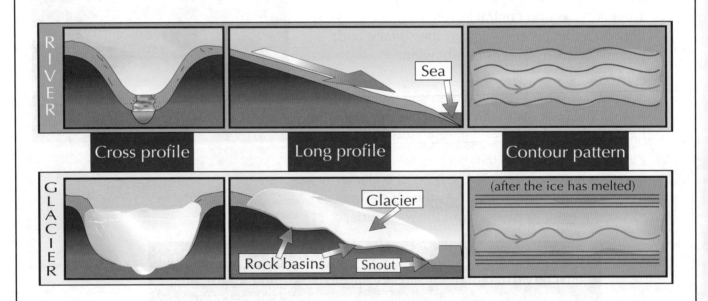

Make a list of the similarities between glaciers and rivers

Remember, these processes have been going on for thousands of years. Try drawing the profiles of the two, it'll help you remember the features of each.

Glacial Erosion

Glacial Erosion created upland features

1) Ice in hollows causes <u>plucking</u> and <u>freeze-thaw action</u> which <u>steepens</u> the back and side walls of the valley.

2) The ice moves with a circular motion which deepens the hollow into a bowl shape called a <u>corrie</u> — forming a lip at the valley end.

3) Once the corrie is <u>full of ice</u> it flows out over the lip and down the valley as a <u>glacier</u>. Where the ice is pulled away from the back wall, a large crevasse is formed.

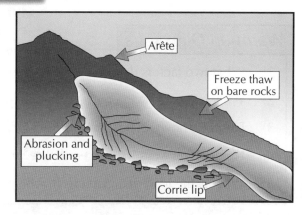

4) When the ice <u>melts</u> it leaves corries — steep-sided, armchair-shaped hollows, often with a <u>tarn</u> (lake) at the bottom — e.g. Red Tarn (Lake District).

5) <u>Two neighbouring corries</u> mean glacial erosion narrows and steepens the wall between them, forming a knife-edged ridge or <u>arête</u> — e.g. Striding Edge on Helvellyn (Lake District).

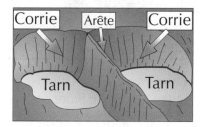

Valley features are Altered by the glacier

1) The valley cross-profile is changed from a <u>V-shape</u> to a <u>U-shape</u> as the glacier moves down it with great power, eroding slope material.

2) The valley, or glacial trough, becomes a <u>straighter</u>, <u>more linear feature</u>, as the ice doesn't wind round spurs but <u>cuts through</u> them, leaving steep edges on the valley sides — <u>truncated spurs</u> — e.g. Nant Ffrancon in Snowdonia is a glaciated valley.

3) <u>Original tributary valleys</u> are now at <u>higher levels</u> than the main valley as they <u>didn't</u> experience such powerful glacial erosion. Tributary streams enter the valley as <u>waterfalls</u> from <u>hanging valleys</u>.

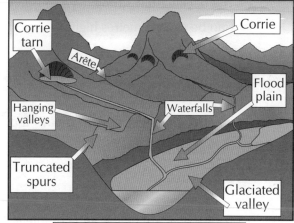

A typical glacial landscape

Glacial erosion had dramatic effects on the landscape

<u>Don't skim</u> this bit, it's easy to get the different features mixed up. And don't go on to the next page until you've got it for definite.

Questions

It's been quite a long section, I know, but rivers, coasts and glaciation are important things and deserve lots of pages. Try the warm up questions first, that'll get your brain going so you can attempt the practice questions.

Warm-up Questions

1) What two factors determine the energy of a wave?

2) What is meant by the term 'fetch' when applied to waves?

3) Describe how: a) beaches, b) spits, c) barrier beaches are formed.

4) Name three ways ice can erode the landscape.

5) What is the load of a glacier? In which three ways do glaciers move their load?

Practice Questions

These practice questions will really help you remember all those facts you just learnt.

1) Draw two columns and write the headings 'constructive waves' and 'destructive waves' at the top. Then write each of the following phrases in the correct column:

    Cause a lot of erosion.

    Cause more deposition than erosion.

    Operate in calmer weather.

    Operate in storm conditions.

    The swash is strong.

    The backwash is strong.

    Can be several metres high.

2) Unscramble the words below to find five ways that the sea erodes the coast. Then explain how each process works.

    a) crudyhila nicota   b) weav pignound

    c) norattiti   d) racoonsir

    e) noisrocro

3) Copy the diagram below and complete it by correctly labelling the erosional features.

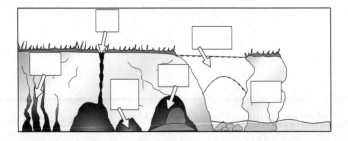

Questions

4) Make two columns with the headings 'hard engineering' and 'soft engineering'.
Then list the flood and erosion control methods from below in their correct columns.

sea walls	**gabions**	**managed retreat**
armour blocks	**revetments**	**shoreline vegetation**
dune stabilisation	**beach nourishment**	**set backs**

5) From the lists you have made, choose a term for each of the following descriptions:

a) Slatted barriers that break the wave force by trapping beach material behind them. They look rather ugly.

b) Instead of spending more and more money on protecting the coast, the sea is allowed to flood into parts of low lying areas.

c) Steel mesh cages full of rocks that absorb some of the wave energy and slow down erosion.

d) Planting of vegetation so that the roots of the plants will hold the beach sediment together.

e) Big mounds of sand are kept in place by planting marram grass and by keeping people to particular footpaths.

6) Look at the diagram below of a glaciated highland landscape.

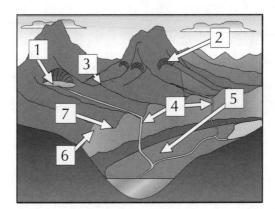

a) Match each number on the diagram with one of the following terms:

Arête	**Corrie**	**Waterfalls**
Corrie tarn	**Hanging valley**	**Flood plain**	**Truncated spur**

b) Explain how this valley was altered and shaped by a glacier. Your description should include an explanation of how the following features arose:

truncated spurs   **hanging valleys**

Section Five — Summary Questions

Phew, that was a huge section. Make sure you can answer all these questions in full — check back in the book when you've finished and fill in any bits you missed. Take a break and then do the whole lot again. When you can do every question without making a mistake, move on to another section.

1) What is the name of the land area from which a river and its tributaries collect the rainwater passing through the soil and rock.

2) Name the following features:
   a) where a river starts
   b) a branch of a main river
   c) where the river flows into the sea (2 possible answers. How are they different?)
   d) the place where two rivers join each other

3) Does a river channel become wider or narrower as it follows its course to the sea?

4) What do the following terms mean when referring to rivers?
   a) load   b) discharge   c) bed   d) velocity   e) banks   f) channel

5) Draw cross- and long-profiles for the upper, middle and lower stages of a river. Add labels to show the differences between them.

6) What are the four ways a river erodes? Describe each briefly.

7) Draw a cross-section of a river meander. Add these labels: river cliff, point bar, strong current, weaker current, deep channel, shallow channel.

8) Describe what flood plains are.

9) Are the effects of flooding likely to be worse in LEDCs or MEDCs?

10) Describe two soft engineering methods of flood management.

11) Draw a labelled diagram to show a wave's crest, trough, length and height.

12) How does a headland and bay coastline form?

13) Describe how a crack in a headland can turn into a stack. Use diagrams to help you.

14) Describe how: a) beaches, b) spits, c) barrier beaches are formed. Give an example of each feature and draw labelled diagrams to show the formation and main features.

15) Describe three main conflicts that may exist between various groups of people in coastal areas.

16) Give four disadvantages of hard engineering techniques.

17) Name five soft engineering approaches to coastal management.

18) What is 'plucking'?

19) Name three ways in which rivers and glaciers are similar.

20) With the aid of a diagram describe the formation and present-day appearance of a corrie in the UK. Mention the processes involved in its formation and label your diagram.

21) What are arêtes? How are they formed? Name an example of one.

22) Draw a diagram to show a glaciated valley. Label the following: hanging valley, truncated spur, waterfall, arête, corrie, tarn.

Population Distribution

Population is the <u>number of people</u> living in a particular place.

Population distribution — *Where People Live*

Population distribution is <u>where</u> people live — this can be on a <u>global</u>, <u>regional</u> or <u>local</u> scale.

1) <u>PLACES WITH LOTS OF PEOPLE</u> usually have habitable environments. They are either:
   - <u>wealthy and industrial</u> e.g. Europe, Japan, Eastern USA.
   - <u>poor</u> with <u>rapidly growing populations</u> e.g. India, Ethiopia.

2) <u>PLACES WITH FEW PEOPLE</u> are usually <u>difficult environments</u> to live in, e.g. Greenland.

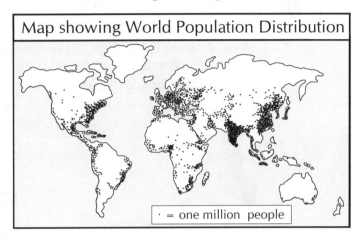

Map showing World Population Distribution

· = one million people

Large Populations *live in* Accessible Areas *with* Good Resources

1) <u>RIVER VALLEYS</u> are <u>sheltered</u>. The river provides a <u>transport</u> and <u>communication link</u> as well as a <u>water supply</u>. Examples: the Ganges Valley in India and the Rhine Valley in Germany.

2) <u>LOWLAND PLAINS</u> are <u>flat with fertile soils</u> allowing productive farming and easy <u>communication</u>. Examples: Denmark — very low lying and famous for dairy products. East Anglia in the UK – a good location for growing cereals.

3) <u>AREAS RICH IN NATURAL RESOURCES</u> can be important sources of materials for <u>industry</u>. Resources include <u>fossil fuels</u> (<u>coal</u>, <u>oil</u> and <u>gas</u>) and <u>ores</u> such as <u>iron</u> and <u>bauxite</u>. An example of an area rich in oil and gas with some highly populated areas is the United Arab Emirates in the Middle East.

4) <u>COASTAL PLAINS</u> often have <u>moderate</u> climates and good access for international <u>trade</u> because they have sea <u>ports</u>. A good example is New York in the USA.

Good communication links, natural resources and hospitable climates

It's no accident that people settle and communities develop in certain areas. Learn the areas where there are dense populations, and the main reasons why people choose those places.

Population Distribution

Few People live in places with Few Resources

 AREAS WITH EXTREME CLIMATES are <u>almost empty</u>. But don't think temperature is the only extreme — lack of precipitation (<u>aridity</u>) is just as important. Humans can cope with pretty hot and cold temperatures but we can't cope without water. Even so, very hot and cold places such as Antarctica and the Sahara Desert are good examples of places too extreme for many people to live in.

The Sahara Desert: too hot and dry for humans, or much else, to live.

Some people have adapted to live in small communities in extreme places like the Inuit in the Arctic Circle.

There are no trees to provide building materials in the Arctic, so igloos can be built from snow and ice.

 HIGH ALTITUDES are <u>inaccessible</u>, have <u>poor soils</u> and <u>steep slopes</u> which means that farming is difficult. This combination means that this environment can support few people. Good examples are the Andes mountains in South America. The inhabitants of the Andes cut terraces into the mountainside to provide strips of flat land to farm.

Terracing in the Andes

Population distribution — it's mostly common sense

There you go then — a couple of starter pages all about where people live and why. A lot of it probably seems pretty obvious but it's got to be done.

Population Density

Population density is a *Measurement* of *People* per *km²*

Population density is the average number of people living in an area — given as people per square kilometre.

Population Density	=	Number of People
		Area

1) A density figure must include a unit of measurement — usually per km².

2) The terms 'densely populated' and 'sparsely populated' are used to refer to areas with high and low population densities.

3) Population density is an average number of people for the area and tells us nothing about where in that area people live. Two places with the same density of population can have very different population distributions.

Map showing World Population Densities

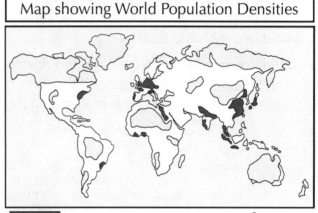

■ = Over 100 people per km²

□ = Less than 1 person per km²

Ideal Population Density gives an Optimum population

The concept of optimum population is about the ideal number of people that can be supported by the resources available. There are only three terms to learn:

Overpopulation — where there are too many people to be supported to a satisfactory level by the resources available.

Underpopulation — where there are too few people to make the most of the resources available.

Optimum Population — where the resources can be used to their best advantage without having too many people to maintain the standard of living.

You can work out Regional Distribution by looking at Densities

This is how the distribution in ASIA varies: Singapore has a density of 8,104 people per km² (try to picture it!) whereas Mongolia's density is just 2 people per km² (2014 figures).

Get your terms straight

You need to get this clear — population density tells us how many people live in an area, population distribution tells us where they live.

Population Growth

The *World's Population* is *Growing* very rapidly

1) The graph below shows <u>world population growth</u>. Note that it is not just the increase that is important, but that <u>the rate of increase has speeded up</u>.

2) The 20th Century saw a <u>population explosion</u>. This means that a dramatic <u>drop</u> in the <u>death rate</u> led to very rapid population growth.

3) <u>Population growth</u> is the result of the balance between <u>birth rate</u>, <u>death rate</u> and <u>migration</u>.

4) The difference between the birth and death rates is the <u>natural increase</u> or <u>natural decrease</u>. (It's '<u>increase</u>' if the birth rate is higher than the death rate and '<u>decrease</u>' if the death rate is higher than the birth rate.)

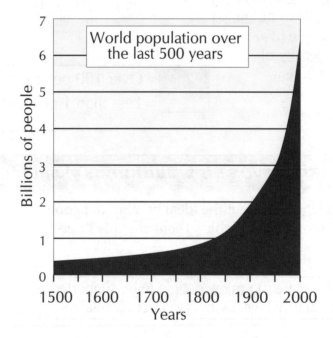

<u>THE BIRTH RATE</u> — the number of <u>live babies born per thousand of the population</u> per year.

<u>THE DEATH RATE</u> — the number of <u>deaths per thousand of the population</u> per year.

<u>MIGRATION</u> — the number of people <u>moving in or out</u>.

Birth, death and migration levels are important for this topic

Make sure this is as clear as crystal before you move on — if more people die than are born the population will go down, if more are born than die it will go up.

Population Growth

Population growth is different in LEDCs (less economically developed countries — i.e. poorer countries) and MEDCs (more economically developed countries — i.e. richer countries).

The **Demographic Transition Model** describes population growth

The population of a country changes over four stages of the demographic transition model. Stage five has been added to show the population decline in some MEDCs like Germany.

Stage 1	Stage 2	Stage 3	Stage 4	Stage 5
High Fluctuating	Early Expanding	Late Expanding	Low Fluctuating	Declining
High birth and death rates cancel each other out: population remains stable and low.	Death rate falls, birth rate remains high: population begins to grow.	Death rate low, birth rate falls: population still rising.	Low birth and death rates cancel each other out: population high but stable.	birth rate drops below death rate: population declining.
E.g. Rainforest tribes 	E.g. Ethiopia 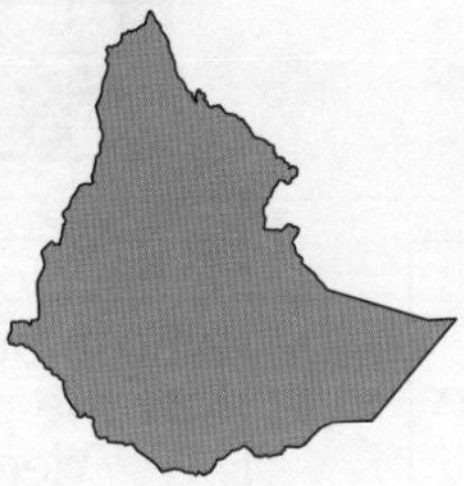	E.g. China 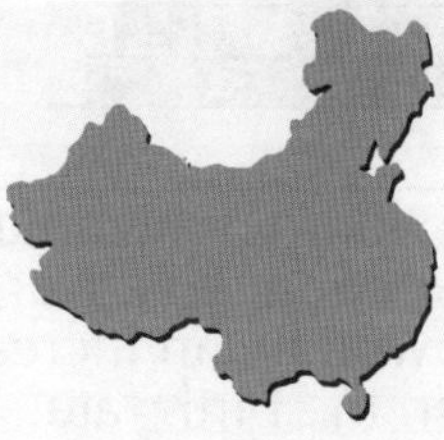	E.g. UK 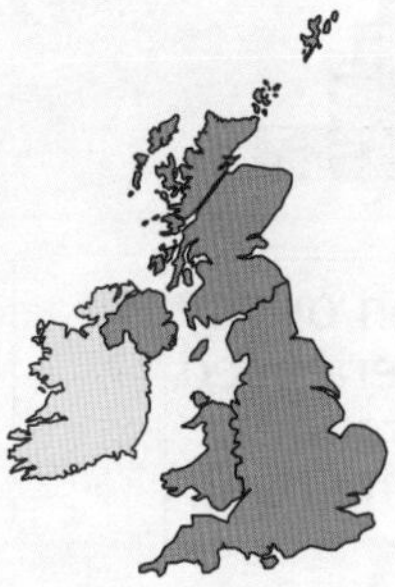	E.g. Germany 

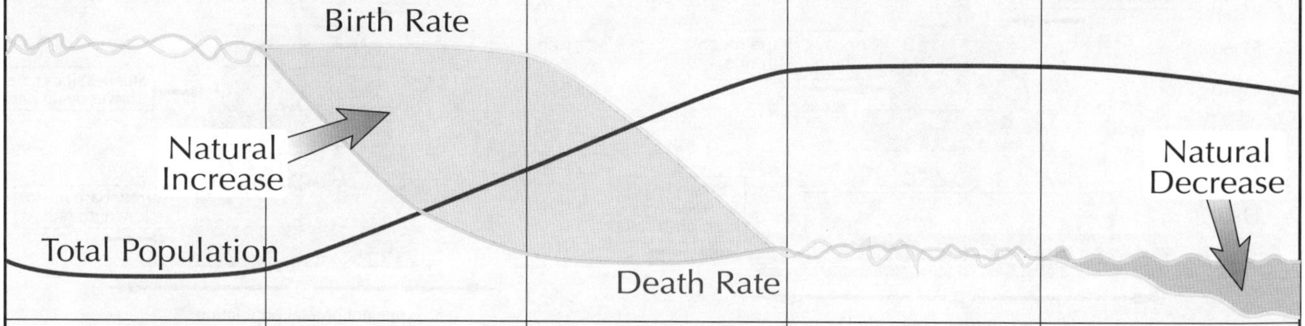

The graph shows Birth Rate, Death Rate, Total Population, Natural Increase and Natural Decrease across the five stages.

Have a long, hard look at it — it gets easier

This one looks tough. It's not that bad. Really. Make some of your own notes on it. Remember that you need to know how to read a graph and interpret what it means — so get learning and practising.

Population Structure

Population structure is the number of <u>males</u> and <u>females</u> in different <u>age groups</u>. It's often shown as a <u>pyramid</u> with males and females on each side and the different ages making up the different sized <u>layers</u>.

Population *Pyramids* show *Population Structure*

1) There are <u>two basic population pyramid shapes</u>.

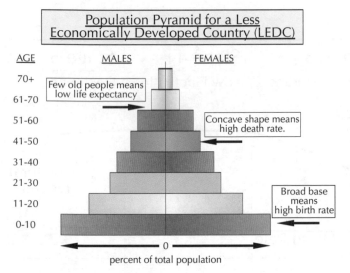

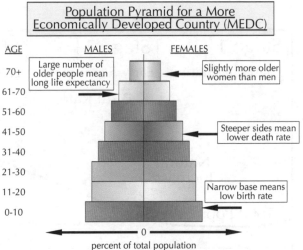

2) There are <u>3 common variations</u> on these basic shapes.

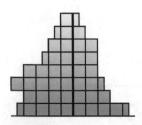

An LEDC region or city which has experienced high in-migration mainly by young men.

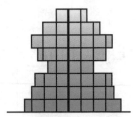

A country which has experienced a war, followed by an increase in the birth rate.

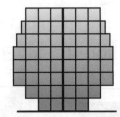

A developed country whose birth rate is so low the population is declining.

The structure of a population is determined by the <u>proportion of males and females</u> and the <u>proportion of people in different age groups</u>.

Migration

These two pages are all about migration — the movement of people. It's not too difficult but there are a few terms to get your head round.

There are **Three Types** of migration

1) <u>International Migration</u> — when people move from one <u>country</u> to another. Remember — this can be across the world, but it can also be a few miles over a border.
2) <u>Regional Migration</u> — when people move between <u>regions</u> within the same country.
3) <u>Local Migration</u> — when people move a <u>short distance</u> within the same region.

Migration can also be **Classified** by **Reason**

Migration happens because of <u>push and pull factors</u>. Learn this diagram to make sure you know the difference. Remember — it's usually a <u>combination</u> of the two that causes migration.

<u>Push factors</u>
These are the things about the <u>origin</u> (where they live) that make someone decide to move. They are usually negative things such as lack of jobs or education opportunities.

<u>Pull factors</u>
These are things about the <u>destination</u> that attract people. They are usually positive things such as job opportunities or the <u>perception</u> of a better standard of living.

Governments play an important role in migration

Governments can either <u>encourage</u> or <u>refuse</u> immigration into their country.
On a local scale, <u>planning and employment</u> policies will affect decisions to move.

Remember, migration isn't just moving from one country to another...

...it can also be moving between regions or areas. Make sure you think about what drives people away from where they are as well as what attracts them to a new place.

Migration

Common types of *Migration* and their *Push And Pull Factors*

1) <u>International migration</u> from LEDCs to MEDCs is usually <u>economic migrants</u> searching for a higher standard of living — e.g. from <u>Mexico</u> to the much <u>wealthier USA</u>.

2) Some international migration is from MEDC to MEDC due to job opportunities or warmer climates — e.g. Britain to Australia. A <u>Brain Drain</u> is when highly qualified people move abroad to better opportunities — e.g. scientists moving from the <u>UK</u> to the <u>USA</u> because researchers are paid far better in the USA.

3) <u>Rural-urban migration</u> is movement from the countryside to the cities, common in LEDCs where facilities and opportunities are greater in urban areas — e.g. Mexican villages to Mexico City.

4) <u>Counter-urbanisation</u> in MEDCs is movement out of cities into rural areas due to a perception of a more relaxed lifestyle, and lower pollution levels. <u>Commuting</u> (living outside the city and travelling in every day to work) has increased this trend.

5) <u>Refugees</u> are people who've been forced to leave their country due to hardship or political oppression. These can be large numbers or individuals — e.g. <u>Kosovans</u> from Albania to the UK because of war in 1999.

See p. 81 for more on rural-urban migration.

So let's be *Clear* about the *Right Terms*

Emigrant
Someone moving
<u>OUT</u> of a country,
region or area.

Migrant
The person doing
the moving.

Immigrant
Someone moving
<u>INTO</u> a country,
region or area.

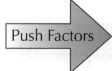
Push Factors

Pull Factors

Learn these two pages together

Remember to get the types of migration clear first — but don't forget the difference between <u>push and pull</u> factors. Try to find a case study in a <u>real</u> place and do a table of push and pull factors.

Questions

Here are two pages of lovely questions for you on the topics covered in the last few pages.

Warm-up Questions

1) Which parts of the world have very few people? Give some examples.
2) Define the term 'population density'. How does it differ from 'distribution'?
3) Define the following terms: Birth Rate, Death Rate, Natural Increase.
4) Draw and label the population pyramids for an LEDC and an MEDC.
5) Describe a variation on the basic shape of a population pyramid.
6) Define these terms: immigrant, migrant, emigrant, refugee.
7) What is counter-urbanisation?

Practice Questions

Take your time with these questions, they're a bit trickier than the warm-up ones.

1) The map shows the distribution of the world's population:

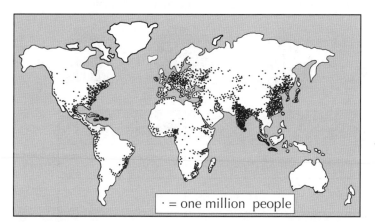

· = one million people

Copy out the following passage. Include the correct words from the pairs.
Give the name of an appropriate country in the spaces.

The population distribution of the world is very **(even / uneven)**. Places with lots of

people include **(wealthy / poor)** industrialised countries, such as _____ ,

_____ and eastern USA and **(wealthy / poor)** countries with

(slowly / rapidly) growing populations such as _____ and

_____. Places with few people are usually **(habitable / hostile)**

environments such as _____.

2) Explain what is meant by the following terms:

    a)   overpopulation

    b)   underpopulation

    c)   optimum population

Questions

3) Copy out the sentences matching the following terms to their correct definition:

natural decrease   **birth rate**   **migration**   **death rate**   **natural increase**

a) The _____ is the number of live babies born per thousand of the population per year.

b) The _____ is the number of deaths per thousand of the population per year.

c) _____ describes people moving into or out of a country.

d) If the birth rate is higher than the death rate, the difference between them is called the _____ .

e) If the death rate is higher than the birth rate, the difference between them is called the _____ .

4) Study the population pyramids below. Match each shape to the place it is most typical of. Put your answers in a copy of the table.

A   B   C   D

Description of Pyramid	Pyramid letter
An MEDC	
An LEDC	
A fast-growing capital city in an LEDC	
An MEDC with a declining population	

5) When talking about migration, describe what is meant by 'push' and 'pull' factors. Give three examples of each.

6) The table below shows terms and descriptions for the movement of people. Copy and complete the table.

Term			Immigrant
Definition	Someone moving out of a country, region or area.	Someone moving from one place to another.	

Urbanisation

Lots of people around the world are <u>moving to urban areas</u> (towns and cities).

*Urbanisation is Happening **Fastest** in **Poorer Countries***

1) <u>Urbanisation</u> is the <u>growth</u> in the <u>number</u> of people living in <u>urban areas</u>.
2) It's happening in countries <u>all over the world</u> — more than <u>50%</u> of the world's population currently live in <u>urban areas</u> (<u>3.4 billion</u> people) and this is <u>increasing</u> every day.
3) But urbanisation <u>differs</u> between <u>richer</u> and <u>poorer</u> countries:

- <u>Most</u> of the population in <u>richer countries</u> <u>already live</u> in <u>urban areas</u>.
- <u>Not many</u> of the population in <u>poorer countries currently live</u> in urban areas.
- Most <u>urbanisation</u> that's happening in the <u>world today</u> is going on in <u>poorer countries</u> and it's happening at a <u>fast pace</u>.

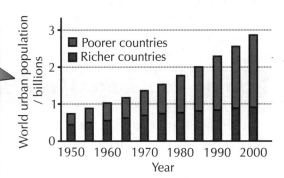

*Urbanisation is **Caused** By **Rural-urban Migration***

1) <u>Rural-urban migration</u> is the movement of people <u>from</u> the <u>countryside</u> to the <u>cities</u>.
2) Rural-urban migration <u>causes</u> urbanisation in <u>richer</u> and <u>poorer countries</u>.
3) The <u>reasons why</u> people move are <u>different</u> in <u>poorer</u> and <u>richer countries</u> though.

> People in <u>poorer countries</u> might move from rural areas to cities because:
> 1) There's often a <u>shortage of services</u> (e.g. education, water and power) in <u>rural areas</u>.
> 2) People from rural areas sometimes <u>believe</u> the <u>standard of living</u> is <u>better</u> in cities.
> 3) There are <u>more jobs</u> in <u>urban areas</u>.
> 4) If <u>harvests fail</u> in rural areas, <u>farmers</u> might have to move to <u>feed</u> their <u>families</u>.

> People in <u>richer countries</u> might move from rural areas to cities because:
> 1) In the past, <u>new factories</u> in urban areas created lots of <u>jobs</u>.
> 2) More recently, <u>run-down</u> inner city areas have been <u>redeveloped</u>, so they are more <u>attractive</u> places to live.

People usually move to cities to look for better jobs and services

Nothing too difficult on this page — richer countries have a <u>high percentage</u> of their population in urban areas, but urbanisation in poorer countries is happening <u>fast</u>.

Urban Issues

Urbanisation can lead to problems — <u>urban areas</u> often have <u>social</u> and <u>environmental issues</u>.

Many Urban Areas Have the Same Problems

Cities in <u>richer countries</u> all have the <u>same kind of problems</u>:

CBD is the Central Business District where all the shops and offices are.

1 A <u>shortage</u> of good quality <u>housing</u>.

2 <u>Run down CBDs</u>.

3 <u>Traffic congestion</u> and <u>pollution</u> from <u>cars</u>.

4 <u>Ethnic segregation</u> (people from different races and religions not mixing).

Growing Populations Need More Housing

Some richer countries (e.g. the UK) have <u>housing shortages</u> in <u>urban areas</u> because the <u>urban population</u> has <u>grown quickly</u>. Here are a few ways the shortages are being <u>tackled</u>:

1) <u>Urban renewal schemes</u>

These are <u>government strategies</u> to <u>encourage investment</u> in <u>new housing</u>, <u>services</u> and <u>employment</u> in <u>derelict inner city areas</u>, e.g. the dockland development in Liverpool.

2) <u>New towns</u>

<u>Brand new towns</u> have been built to house the <u>overspill populations</u> from existing towns and cities where there was a <u>shortage of housing</u>. E.g. Milton Keynes is a new town built in the 1970s.

3) <u>Relocation incentives</u>

These are used to <u>encourage</u> people living in <u>large council houses</u> (who <u>don't really need</u> a <u>big house</u> or to <u>live in the city</u>) to <u>move out</u> of urban areas. This <u>frees up houses</u> in urban areas for other people, e.g. <u>working families</u>.

Efforts are being Made to Revitalise CBDs

The <u>CBDs</u> in some cities are <u>run down</u>. One reason for this is competition from <u>out-of-town shopping centres</u> and <u>business parks</u>, which have <u>cheaper rent</u> and <u>are easier to drive to</u>. But steps are being taken to <u>revitalise</u> some CBDs and <u>attract people back</u> to them. For example:

1) <u>Pedestrianising</u> areas (stopping car access) to make them <u>safer</u> and <u>nicer for shoppers</u>.
2) <u>Improving access</u>, with <u>better public transport links</u> and <u>better car parking</u>.
3) <u>Converting</u> derelict warehouses and docks into <u>smart</u> new shops, restaurants and museums.
4) <u>Improving public areas</u>, e.g. parks and squares, to make them <u>more attractive</u>.

Urban Issues

Increased Car Use has an Impact on Urban Environments

There are <u>more and more cars</u> on the roads of cities in richer countries. This causes
a variety of <u>problems</u>, which can <u>discourage</u> people from visiting and shopping in the city:

1 More air pollution,
which damages
health

2 More road
accidents

3 Air pollution also
damages buildings

4 More traffic jams
and congestion

There are a variety of <u>solutions</u> to help <u>reduce traffic</u> and its <u>impacts</u>:

1) <u>Improving public transport</u> to <u>encourage</u> people to use cars <u>less</u>.

2) <u>Increasing car parking charges</u> in city centres to <u>discourage</u> people from using their
   cars, and use <u>public transport</u> instead.

3) <u>Bus priority lanes</u> — these <u>speed up bus services</u> so people are <u>more likely to use them</u>.

4) <u>Pedestrianisation</u> of central areas. This <u>removes traffic</u> from the main shopping streets,
   which <u>reduces</u> the number of <u>accidents</u> and <u>pollution levels</u>.

Many Urban Areas Have a Variety of Cultures

Cities usually have a <u>variety</u> of people from different <u>ethnic backgrounds</u> (people from
different <u>races</u> and <u>religions</u>). But there's often <u>ethnic segregation</u> in urban areas, i.e.
people of different ethnicities not mixing. There are several <u>reasons</u> for this, for example:

1) People <u>prefer</u> to <u>live close</u> to others with the <u>same background</u> and <u>religion</u>,
   and who speak the <u>same language</u>.

2) People <u>live near</u> to <u>services</u> that are <u>important</u> to <u>their culture</u>, e.g. <u>places of worship</u>.
   This means people of the <u>same ethnic background</u> tend to <u>live</u> in the <u>same area</u>.

Strategies to support mulitcultural areas are about making sure that everyone has equal
<u>access</u> to <u>services</u> like <u>health care</u> and <u>education</u>. For example:

1) Making sure <u>everyone</u> can <u>access information</u> about the different <u>services</u>
   e.g. by printing leaflets in a variety of languages.

2) <u>Improving communication</u> between all parts of the community, e.g. by <u>involving</u>
   the <u>leaders</u> of <u>different ethnic communities</u> when <u>making decisions</u>.

Public transport, parking charges and pedestrianisation can help

All this stuff seems pretty straightforward but keep going over it until it's all lodged in your
brain. Cover the page and try to remember the problems and the solutions.

Squatter Settlements

Squatter settlements are found in lots of big cities in poorer countries — people live there if they have nowhere else to go.

Squatter Settlements are Common in Cities in Poorer Countries

1) Squatter settlements are settlements that are built illegally in and around the city, by people who can't afford proper housing.

2) Squatter settlements are a problem in many growing cities in poorer countries, e.g. São Paulo (Brazil) and Mumbai (India).

3) Most of the inhabitants have moved to the city from the countryside — they're rural–urban migrants.

4) The settlements are badly built and overcrowded.

Little space between houses

No electricity or phone lines

Houses built from waste material like plastic sheets

©iStockphoto.com/Holger Mette

No paved roads or sewers

1) Life in a squatter settlement can be hard and dangerous — there's often no clean running water, sewers or electricity and no policing or medical services.

2) Because of these problems, life expectancy is often very low.

3) Many inhabitants within the settlements work long hours for little pay.

There are Ways to Improve Squatter Settlements

People living in squatter settlements usually try to improve the settlements themselves. But the residents have little money and can achieve much more with a bit of help:

SELF-HELP SCHEMES — these involve the government and local people working together to make improvements. E.g. the government supply building materials and local people use them to build their own homes.

SITE AND SERVICE SCHEMES — people pay a small amount of rent for a site, and they can borrow money to build or improve their house. The rent money is then used to provide basic services for the area.

LOCAL AUTHORITY SCHEMES — these are funded by the local government and are about improving the temporary accommodation built by residents.

Squatter settlements are sometimes called slums or shanty towns

Life in a squatter settlement is pretty tough. But people who live in them try to improve the conditions themselves, and there are usually government schemes to help them too.

Urbanisation Environmental Issues

Rapid urbanisation in poorer countries brings a whole host of environmental problems...

Rapid Urbanisation can Affect the Environment

Rapid urbanisation can cause a number of environmental problems:

1) Waste disposal problems — people in cities create a lot of waste. This can damage people's health and the environment.
2) More air pollution from burning fuel, vehicle exhaust fumes and factories.
3) More water pollution — water carries pollutants from cities into rivers and streams.

Waste Disposal is a Serious Problem in Poorer Countries

In richer countries, waste is disposed of by burying it in landfill sites, or by burning it. The amount of waste is also reduced by recycling schemes. Poorer countries struggle to dispose of the large amount of waste that's created by rapid urbanisation for many reasons:

1) Money — poorer countries often can't afford to dispose of waste safely. There are often more urgent problems to spend limited funds on, e.g. healthcare.
2) Infrastructure — poorer countries don't have the infrastructure needed, e.g. poor roads in squatter settlements mean waste disposal lorries can't get in to collect rubbish.
3) Scale — the problem is huge. A large city will generate thousands of tonnes of waste every day.

Air and Water Pollution Have Many Effects

Air pollution
- Air pollution can lead to acid rain, which damages buildings and vegetation.
- It can cause health problems like headaches and bronchitis.
- Some pollutants destroy the ozone layer, which protects us from the sun's harmful rays.

Water pollution
- Water pollution kills fish and other aquatic animals, which disrupts food chains.
- Harmful chemicals can build up in the food chain and poison humans who eat fish from the polluted water.
- Contamination of water supplies with sewage can spread diseases like typhoid.

Managing air and water pollution costs a lot of money and requires lots of different resources. This makes it harder for poorer countries to manage pollution.

Poorer countries can't afford to dispose of all their waste properly

Many poor countries don't have any regulations to stop air and water pollution, or their regulations aren't enforced — either way, this leads to environmental problems.

Questions

It's time to look back at what you've learnt about urbanisation.
Have a go at the questions below.

Warm-up Questions

1) Give a definition of urbanisation.

2) What is rural-urban migration?

3) Give one reason why ethnic segregation happens in cities.

4) Name a city where squatter settlements have become a problem.

5) Name three schemes that can help improve squatter settlements.

Practice Questions

These questions might take a little longer to complete, but it's all good practice.

1) Copy and complete the passage below using the correct choice of words.

Urbanisation is the growth in the **(number / weight)** of people living in **(rural / urban)** areas. **(More / Less)** than 50% of the world's population currently live in urban areas. Most of the population in **(richer / poorer)** countries already live in urban areas. Urbanisation is caused by **(urban-rural / rural-urban)** migration.

2) Write down two reasons why:

a) people in poorer countries might move from rural areas to cities.

b) people in richer countries might move from rural areas to cities.

3) Copy out and complete the sentences, adding the correct words from the list below:

urban renewal schemes　　　　　　**large council houses**

shortage of housing　　　　**frees up houses**　　　　**overspill populations**

a) Relocation incentives are used to encourage people living in _____ (who don't need them) to move out of urban areas. This _____ in urban areas for other people.

b) Brand new towns have been built to house the _____ from existing towns and cities where there was a _____.

c) _____ are government schemes to encourage investment in new housing, services and employment in derelict inner city areas.

Questions

4) Write out the actions below which would help to revitalise a run down CBD.

   a) Improve access to the city centre, making public transport links and car parking better.

   b) Close down some shops to make the streets quieter.

   c) Improve public areas, e.g. parks, to make them more attractive.

   d) Create TV adverts promoting rural regions.

   e) Convert derelict warehouses into smart shops, restaurants and museums.

   f) Pedestrianise areas to make them safer and nicer for shops.

5) Describe what a squatter settlement is and explain why
   life can be hard and dangerous for people who live in them.

6) Copy and complete the table below to describe how the following schemes
   can help to improve squatter settlements:

Scheme	How it works
Self-help scheme	
Site & service scheme	
	These are funded by the local government and are about improving the temporary accommodation built by residents.

7) Air pollution and water pollution can be caused by rapid urbanisation.
   Copy and complete the diagram below, writing in two effects of each form of pollution.

   Air pollution
   1._____
   2._____

   Water pollution
   1._____
   2._____

Section Six — Summary Questions

Behold the first 'human geography' section of the book. Instead of the cold hard facts of physical geography, human geography has theories, trends and lots of technical terms. There are fewer fancy diagrams to learn, but lots of tricky phrases. Have a crack at this lot, mark 'em, correct 'em and do them all again until it's sorted.

1) Which parts of the world have lots of people? Explain why and give some examples.

2) Give two reasons why river valleys are densely populated. Name two examples.

3) Why are high altitude areas sparsely populated?

4) Define the terms 'overpopulation', 'underpopulation' and 'optimum population'.

5) Sketch a graph of the world's population over the last 500 years.

6) Explain what 'natural increase' and 'natural decrease' mean.

7) Name one country for stages 2, 3, 4 and 5 (there are no countries at stage 1 any more) of the demographic transition model.

8) Make a list of the population characteristics that can be identified in a population pyramid.

9) Draw a population pyramid for an MEDC.

10) Draw and label a population pyramid shape for each of the following:

a) An LEDC city or region which has experienced high in-migration especially by young men.

b) A country that has experienced war followed by an increase in the birth rate.

c) A developed country whose birth rate is so low the population is declining.

11) What are the three types of migration?

12) What is a 'push' factor? Give two examples.

13) What is a 'pull' factor? Give two examples.

14) Is urbanisation happening more rapidly in poorer or richer countries?

15) List three problems caused by urbanisation in richer countries.

16) Give two ways a city might try to revitalise a CBD.

17) Give two impacts that increased car use can have on urban environments.

18) Give two other names for squatter settlements.

19) Urbanisation can cause air pollution. Describe where this air pollution might come from.

20) Describe the effects of air pollution and water pollution caused by urbanisation.

Contrasts in Development

Development is the process of a country getting wealthier and improving standards of living.

The World's Wealth is not shared out equally

The world can be divided into richer and poorer countries — 20% of the world's population live in MEDCs and own 80% of the world's wealth.

1) Wealthier countries are known as More Economically Developed Countries or MEDCs.

2) Poorer countries are described as Less Economically Developed Countries or LEDCs — they're also called Developing Countries or the Third World. This term came from a time when MEDCs were known as the First World, the former Communist countries were the Second World, and the rest were the Third World.

3) The term development refers to how mature a country's economy, infrastructure and social systems are — the more developed a country's economic systems are, the wealthier it is.

> GNI per capita =
> Gross National Income
> per capita — see page 90

4) The Development Gap is the contrast between rich and poor countries. It's best shown by example — in 2012 the estimated GNI per capita of Switzerland was 80 970 US Dollars; for Tanzania it was 570 US Dollars.

Developed and developing worlds — the North-South Divide

The map of rich and poor countries can be split by a line called the North-South Divide.

1) The richer countries are almost all in the northern hemisphere — except Australia and New Zealand.

2) Poorer countries are mostly in the tropics and the southern hemisphere.

3) Places that suffer from natural disasters like droughts and cyclones are often developing countries.

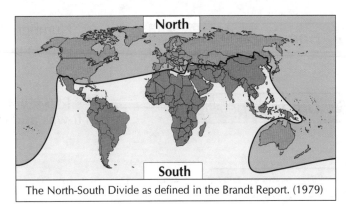

The North-South Divide as defined in the Brandt Report. (1979)

4) The richer countries mainly have temperate (moderate) climates and good natural resources — there are exceptions, like Japan, which has few natural resources.

5) The explanations for the North-South Divide have as much to do with political history as they do with physical geography. Many MEDCs had colonies in LEDCs and there are still restrictions imposed on world trade — this means the development gap is getting wider.

There are (of course) exceptions to the North-South rule

Australia and New Zealand are in the southern hemisphere but they're still MEDCs. Japan is an MEDC but has few natural resources. There's no alternative but to learn them off by heart.

Measuring Development

Geographers like to measure how developed a country is so that it's easier to compare countries.

Development Indicators show How Developed a country is

The concept of LEDCs and MEDCs is fairly straightforward, but measuring a country's development is more complicated, because there are so many indicators of development.

1. Gross Domestic Product (GDP)

This is the total value of goods and services a country produces in a year. Gross National Income (GNI) is similar but includes money from people of that nationality living abroad. This is often used but it says nothing about distribution of wealth — it can therefore be misleading. (GNI per capita is total value of goods and services produced in a year per person.)

2. Life expectancy

The average age a person can expect to live to — it's usually higher for women.

3. Infant mortality rate

Number of babies who die under 1 year old, per thousand live births.

4. Calorie intake

The average number of calories eaten per day — an average adult woman needs around 2000 to stay healthy.

5. Energy consumption

Number of British thermal units (Btu) used per person per year — an indication of level of industry.

6. Urban population

The percentage of the total population living in towns and cities.

7. Literacy rates

Percentage of adults who can read enough to 'get by'.

8. Number of people per doctor

The number of potential patients for every doctor.

Many of these indicators are linked, and *relationships* can be identified — for example countries with high GDP tend to have high urban populations and consume a lot of energy. These relationships can also be used to identify a country's level of development.

Development indicators — read it until you know it

There are quite a few indicators to remember here — close the book, grab a bit of paper and scribble down the eight listed above. Don't worry if you can't get them all first time.

Measuring Development

Here's an example to help you understand...

Development indicators — *Comparing* development levels

Development indicators are statistics that can be <u>quantified</u> — expressed as numbers — and therefore easily <u>compared</u>. Common indicators are shown below comparing the UK and Ethiopia.

		_UK_	_Ethiopia_
	1. **GNI per capita**	$38,500	$380
	2. **Life expectancy**	women 84 yrs men 80 yrs	women 65 yrs men 61 yrs
	3. **Infant mortality rate**	5 per thousand	68 per thousand
	4. **Calorie intake**	Over 3,000 per day	Under 2,000 per day
	5. **Energy consumption**	142 million Btu per person per year	1.56 million Btu per person per year
	6. **Urban population**	80%	17%
	7. **Literacy rates**	99%	39%
	8. **Number of people per doctor**	361	33,333

Two main *Problems* with *Indicators*

1) Some countries may <u>appear</u> to be developed according to some indices but not others — as a country develops, some aspects develop <u>before</u> others. No measurement should be used on its own — it should be <u>balanced</u> with something else to avoid any inaccuracies.

2) Up to date information <u>isn't</u> always <u>available</u> — because a country <u>doesn't have</u> the <u>administration</u> necessary to compile and publish it, or because they <u>don't want</u> the information to be available publicly. This can make <u>comparisons</u> between countries <u>difficult</u>.

You need to be able to interpret statistics on development levels

Development indicators are used as a way of measuring development — but the system's not perfect all the time — so it's worth remembering those two problem points.

Obstacles to Development

Many LEDCs have significant <u>environmental</u> and <u>health problems</u> that slow down the development process.

Natural Hazards cause Development Problems in LEDCs

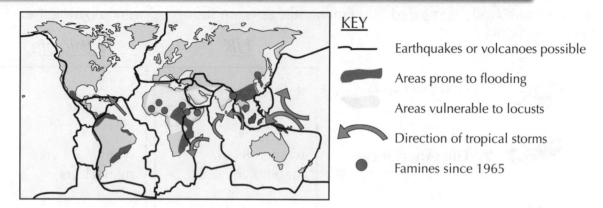

KEY

— Earthquakes or volcanoes possible

Areas prone to flooding

Areas vulnerable to locusts

Direction of tropical storms

● Famines since 1965

1) <u>Drought</u> is a problem in some LEDCs and threatens farming.

2) <u>Tropical storms</u> (also called hurricanes, typhoons and cyclones) are common in Asia and the Caribbean and <u>destroy</u> crops and buildings — repair costs can be enormous.

3) <u>Flooding</u> causes damage to crops, buildings and infrastructure. In Asia, <u>monsoon winds</u> bring <u>heavy rain</u>, which regularly causes <u>flooding</u>.

4) Other <u>natural hazards</u> like <u>earthquakes</u>, <u>volcanoes</u>, and <u>tsunamis</u> (big waves) cause major damage in many LEDCs. <u>Poor warning</u> and <u>prediction systems</u> lead to many <u>deaths</u> and lots of <u>damage</u> to property. Farmland and development schemes can be destroyed or set back.

5) <u>Pests</u>, e.g. locusts, are also common in some LEDCs and can devastate crops in hours.

6) LEDCs often have <u>extreme climates</u> that make it really difficult to develop because money is spent on surviving in this climate rather than on developing resources.

Poor Health and Disease also Hold Back Development

LEDCs often have high levels of disease and general poor health due to a number of factors:

1) <u>Poor diet</u> leads to <u>malnutrition</u> and diseases such as rickets and kwashiorkor — a condition affecting children.

2) <u>Bad sanitation</u> results in <u>polluted water</u> (from human faeces getting into the drinking water), and this can lead to a high level of <u>water-borne diseases</u> such as typhoid and cholera.

3) <u>Tropical diseases</u> like malaria are common in some LEDCs — the tropical climate in these countries is perfect for the <u>mosquito</u> that carries malaria.

4) There are high levels of <u>Sexually Transmitted Infections</u> (STIs) in LEDCs because the population is not educated about how to prevent them spreading. Recently, <u>AIDS</u> has been an increasing concern, especially in Africa.

Improving health is part of development but severe health problems like those found in LEDCs use up a lot of a country's development budget.

Money that could be used for development is needed for other things...

...like rebuilding roads after earthquakes, feeding the population when drought has ruined all their crops and generally surviving in difficult climates — the list is endless...

Obstacles to Development

The colonial history of LEDCs and MEDCs also helps explain the North-South Divide.

The **Colonial Period** established **World Trade Patterns**

1) In the 18th and 19th centuries, the Developing World was colonised by European countries — the colonisers began by setting up trading posts but soon took control of whole territories.

2) Colonies provided agricultural produce not available in Europe, and were a cheap source of raw materials for European industry.

3) Colonial countries provided a market for European goods. The Europeans made sure that their own colonies bought their goods — often at the expense of industry in the colony itself.

Now the colonisers are all MEDCs (e.g. Britain, France and Spain) and the colonies are mostly LEDCs. This pattern of trade still exists today. LEDCs produce raw materials, which mainly MEDCs buy. The MEDCs produce manufactured products that they sell to LEDCs.

However, some people think that this pattern of trade makes LEDCs dependent on MEDCs.

An **Example** of the **Colonial Trade Pattern** — the **UK** and **India**

<u>UK</u>
Cotton was brought from India to mills in Lancashire — India was a cheap source of raw cotton. The British textile industry grew as a result. Cloth sold to India at a higher price than the cotton was bought for — profit made.

<u>INDIA</u>
Cotton bought at low prices and shipped to England. India forced to buy cloth from England at higher prices. The Indian textile industry could not grow as a result.

Some LEDCs **Can't Develop** due to **Debt**

1) Many LEDCs tried to break free of the dependency cycle by borrowing money to finance development.

2) When interest rates rose in the 1980s, they couldn't repay these debts.

3) Rising debts mean many LEDCs have no money to invest in agriculture and industry, so development slows down. Some people think the only way out of the cycle is for lenders to cancel the debts.

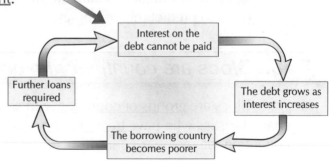

Interest on the debt cannot be paid

The debt grows as interest increases

The borrowing country becomes poorer

Further loans required

4) In the late 1990s, some MEDCs started cancelling some of the debt on humanitarian grounds, but most LEDCs still have a lot of debt to pay back.

5) However, some people think it's unfair for one country to borrow a lot of money from another and never pay it back.

World trade patterns follow colonial trade patterns

This is a history page, and a really important one for you to understand. It tells you why world trade patterns have turned out like they have. These trade patterns are another reason why some LEDCs find it hard to develop — don't forget the others though, e.g. climate and health.

World Trade

Trade is the exchange of goods and services between countries. World trade patterns are an important aspect of development — seriously influencing a country's economy.

World Trade Patterns benefit *MEDCs* more than *LEDCs*

LEDCs have a relatively small share of world trade, and rely heavily on primary products for export earnings.

Primary Products have four *Disadvantages* for *LEDCs*

1) Raw materials have less value than manufactured goods.

2) Prices are dictated by the MEDC buyers, not the producing countries.

3) Prices fluctuate yearly and prediction is difficult.

4) Man-made alternatives to some raw materials reduce demand — e.g. the use of polyester for clothing has reduced the demand for cotton; plastics reduce demand for rubber.

MEDCs rely on *Manufactured Goods*

Manufactured goods have a higher value than primary products, and hold steady prices. The graph shows the effect of this and there are two important points to notice:

1) The price of manufactured goods is rising faster so the gap between the prices of manufactured goods and raw materials is widening — rich countries get richer and poor countries, relatively poorer.

2) Prices of manufactured goods are steady, while raw materials often fluctuate. This makes it difficult for LEDCs to predict their earnings.

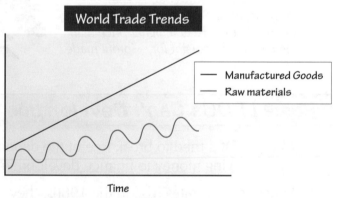

Trade Blocs are countries who are *Trading Partners*

1) Trade blocs are groups of countries with similar characteristics who have trade agreements benefiting the member countries.

— e.g. the EU and NAFTA (North American Free Trade Agreement).

2) An important feature of trade blocs is that member states don't charge tariffs on trade with each other, to encourage trade within the group. This means that LEDCs not in a trade bloc find it hard to export their goods.

— tariffs are taxes levied on imports to make them more expensive than domestically produced goods. They are higher for manufactured goods than for raw materials.

World trade patterns and trade blocs determine who trades with who

This page isn't too difficult — LEDCs sell mostly raw materials and MEDCs sell mostly manufactured products. Also, some countries are in trade blocs to benefit each other.

Aid

Aid is giving resources — goods or services — usually from MEDCs to LEDCs, either in an emergency or to promote long-term development.

Aid can be *Bilateral*, *Multilateral* or *Non-Governmental*

1) Bilateral aid is aid given directly from one government to another — it could be money, training, personnel, technology, food and other supplies.

2) Multilateral aid is aid given through an agency such as the World Bank, usually money. The agency then distributes the aid to countries that need it.

3) Non-Governmental aid is given through organisations like charities — e.g. Oxfam, Save the Children or VSO (Voluntary Service Overseas). This type of aid is very varied, and can include small-scale development projects as well as emergency help where there is a disaster.

Arguments *In Favour* of giving *Aid*

1) Emergency aid in times of disaster has saved lives and reduced people's misery.

2) Development projects, such as provision of clean water, can lead to long-term improvements to living standards.

3) Assistance in developing natural resources and power supplies benefits the economy.

4) Aiding industrial development can create jobs and improve the infrastructure (e.g. roads, electricity supplies).

5) Aid for agriculture can help to increase the food supply.

6) Provision of medical training and equipment can improve health and standards of living.

Arguments *Against* giving *Aid*

1) Aid can increase the dependency of LEDCs on the donor country.

2) Profit from large projects can go to MNCs (Multi National Companies) and donors, rather than the country that is supposed to be receiving the aid.

3) Aid doesn't always reach the people who need it and can be kept by corrupt officials.

4) Aid can be spent on 'prestige projects' (see p.96) or in urban areas rather than in areas of real need.

5) Aid can be used as a weapon to exert political pressure on the receiving country.

Donor country = the country giving aid

The poorest countries don't always get the most aid. Some MEDCs help LEDCs for political purposes — the USA helps the Philippines in return for a strategic location for military bases.

Aid isn't always used appropriately

There's a lot of information here. Giving aid is a complicated issue, but whether you worry about it or not, you still need to know the arguments for and against it.

Development Projects

Development projects are schemes promoting development in LEDCs — often funded by aid money. They range from huge multi-million dollar schemes to small self-help projects.

Large-scale prestige projects *Don't Always Succeed*

1) Some governments opt for <u>prestige projects</u> — expensive, well-publicised schemes like dams providing water and electricity for large areas. Famous examples include the Aswan Dam in Egypt and the Gezira irrigation scheme in Sudan.

2) Prestige projects can be <u>successful</u>, but often they <u>fail</u> to achieve their aims. Some of the problems are outlined in the diagram here.

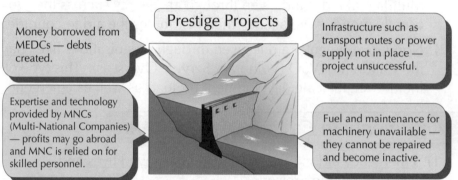

Prestige Projects

Money borrowed from MEDCs — debts created.

Expertise and technology provided by MNCs (Multi-National Companies) — profits may go abroad and MNC is relied on for skilled personnel.

Infrastructure such as transport routes or power supply not in place — project unsuccessful.

Fuel and maintenance for machinery unavailable — they cannot be repaired and become inactive.

Small-scale Projects can lead to *Long-term* development

Small-scale projects are <u>government</u> or <u>charity-funded</u>. They provide <u>specific improvements</u> for a small area and prioritise <u>training</u> for local people — this means they become <u>self-sufficient</u>, needing no outside help.

There are *Three Main Categories* of small-scale project

1) Provision of <u>basic necessities</u> to improve <u>standards of living</u>, such as clean water and sanitation, safe storage of agricultural produce or road building.

2) Provision of <u>essential services</u> such as a health clinic or a school.

3) Setting up co-operatives to facilitate <u>low cost borrowing</u> and <u>saving schemes</u> run by local people to allow investment in agriculture or employment.

Small-scale projects have several advantages:

SMALL-SCALE PROJECTS

Costs are lower and do not incur large debts.

Local people have ownership of the project and do not have to rely on outsiders.

Training has long term benefits for local people.

Appropriate technology is used and maintenance is less of a problem.

Development projects — small is usually best

There you are then, two sizes of development projects and three types of small-scale projects — you've really got to learn the lot. Remember — big projects can help lots of people but they're more <u>risky</u>. Smaller projects have a <u>higher success rate</u> but help <u>fewer people</u>.

Questions

That section wasn't too bad — you need to learn how development is measured, why some countries are more developed than others (i.e. reasons for the North-South Divide) and how aid and development projects try to increase development in LEDCs.

Warm-up Questions

1) What do MEDC and LEDC stand for?

2) List the eight indicators of development. What are the two problems with the indicators?

3) Suggest two arguments in favour of giving aid.

4) What are the four big problems with large-scale prestige development projects?

Practice Questions

Now that you're warmed up you'll have no trouble with these practice questions... enjoy.

1) Copy and complete this sentence about development using the correct words from the pairs:

The 20% of the world's population who live in (**MEDCs / LEDCs**)

own (**80% / 50%**) of the world's wealth.

2) Write out this paragraph about the North-South Divide, choosing words from the box to fill in the spaces.

southern	**developing**	**Japan**
New Zealand	**North**	**hemisphere**
West	**area**	**developed**

The _____-South Divide separates developed from developing

countries. The _____ countries are all in the northern

_____, except for Australia and_____.

Poor countries are mostly in the tropics and the _____ hemisphere.

3) Copy and complete the table to show what these terms mean:

Development Indicator	Meaning
Life expectancy	
Infant mortality rate	
Calorie intake	
Energy consumption	
Literacy rate	

Questions

4) Why can it be difficult to compare countries using development indicators?

5) Look at the map. Name the natural hazards that are a problem in the places listed below it (there may be more than one for each place).

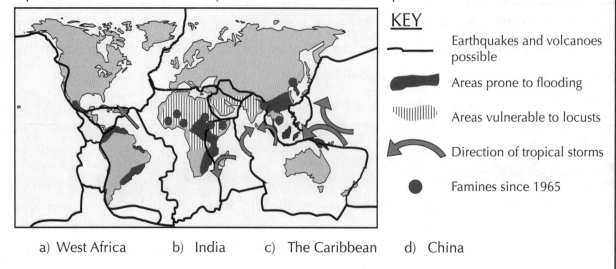

KEY

——— Earthquakes and volcanoes possible

◣ Areas prone to flooding

||||||||| Areas vulnerable to locusts

⤶ Direction of tropical storms

● Famines since 1965

   a) West Africa   b) India   c) The Caribbean   d) China

6) Relying on selling primary goods for income causes four main problems for LEDCs. Describe why each of the following causes problems:

   a) The value of raw materials

   b) MEDCs decide prices

   c) Fluctuation of prices

   d) Man-made alternatives to raw materials

7) Copy out this paragraph about aid, using the correct options from the pairs.

   Aid is the giving of (**resources / responsibilities**) from one country to another.

   It is usually given from (**more / less**) economically developed countries to

   (**more / less**) economically developed countries.

8) Explain what is meant by these terms:

   a) bilateral aid

   b) multilateral aid

   c) non-governmental aid

9) Write a definition of 'development projects'.

10) Answer these questions about small-scale development projects:

   a) How are small-scale projects funded?

   b) How do self-help projects help local people to become self-sufficient?

Section Seven — Summary Questions

Time to see what you've learned and what you need to go over again. Keep at it — I know it's hard work, but it's all important stuff.

1) On the world map below, draw a line showing the North South Divide.

2) Are the poorer countries mostly in the north or the south?

3) Give three examples of MEDCs.

4) Give three examples of LEDCs.

5) Why can GDP be misleading as an indicator of development?

6) Look at the following table. It shows some statistics for Japan, Bangladesh and Brazil (1995). Which of these three countries are A, B and C?

Country	GDP per capita $	Life expectancy	Literacy rate	% Urban pop
A	29,387	80	99	77.6
B	208	56	38	18.3
C	2,528	66	83	78.2

7) Write a paragraph to explain how natural hazards cause development problems in LEDCs.

8) How do health problems hold back the development of LEDCs?

9) Write a paragraph to explain the influence of the colonial era on the present location of developed and developing countries. You should include the colonial influence on world trade patterns.

10) Give two reasons why it is better to rely on manufactured goods rather than raw materials as exports.

11) What is a trade bloc?

12) Give examples of two trade blocs.

13) Write a paragraph to explain how MEDCs have the advantage in world trade.

14) Draw a table to show the advantages and disadvantages of giving aid. (Include three disadvantages and three advantages.)

15) What are the four advantages of small-scale projects?

Classification of Industry

These two pages are all about <u>different types of industry</u>. Oh, the excitement...
it's almost too much.

There are **Four Types** of **Industry**

1) **Primary** industry involves **Raw Materials**

<u>Raw materials</u> are anything <u>naturally present</u> in or on the Earth <u>before</u> processing.
They are collected in three ways:

i)   They can be <u>quarried</u>, <u>mined</u> or <u>drilled for</u> below the Earth's surface
— for example coal mining, oil drilling, limestone quarrying.

ii) They can be <u>grown</u> — farming and forestry are both primary industries.

iii) They can be <u>collected</u> from the sea — fishing is also a primary industry.

Primary industry, such as oil extraction and fishing

2) **Secondary** industry is **Manufacturing** a product

A <u>product</u> from <u>primary industry</u> is turned into <u>another product</u>. But the <u>finished product</u> of one secondary industry may be <u>raw material</u> for another.

For example, one factory may make tyres which are then sent to be used in a car plant.

Secondary industry, such as oil refining and fishing processing

---

Primary = raw materials, secondary = manufacturing products

Make sure you're comfortable with primary and secondary industry before you move on.
This stuff is essential to this section, so learn it well.

Classification of Industry

3) *Tertiary* industry provides a *Service*

This involves a wide <u>range</u> of services <u>instead</u> of making anything, and is the <u>largest</u> group of industries in <u>MEDCs</u>. Examples are anything from teaching, nursing and retail to the police force or the civil service and transport.

Tertiary industry, such as a petrol station or fish restaurant

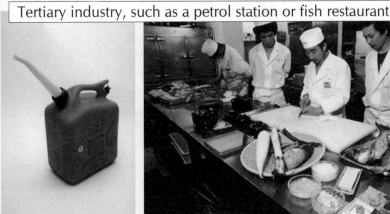

4) *Quaternary* industry involves a small group of

Research and *Development* industries

It's the <u>newest</u> industrial sector and is growing rapidly due to developments in <u>information technology</u> and <u>communication</u>.

Quaternary industry — scientists are employed for research

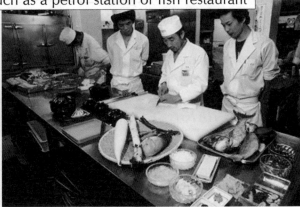

Industry is *not* the same as *Employment*

<u>Employment</u> is the <u>job of work</u> you do. So you could have a tertiary job as a secretary in a secondary industry like a toy factory.
Remember that <u>industries</u> are often <u>connected together</u>, e.g. farmers grow crops, which are processed by companies in the secondary sector.

Don't get industry confused with employment

Remember that quaternary industry is less common than the others — it <u>doesn't</u> have to be part of the process unless the company needs new research.

Location of Industry

This page describes the <u>four</u> big influences on the location of industry — <u>raw materials</u>, <u>labour supply</u>, <u>transport</u> and <u>the market</u>.

Raw Materials influence Industrial Location

1) Locating <u>near</u> raw materials <u>reduces transport costs</u>, particularly if they are bulky or lose weight during the manufacturing process, e.g. a cement works will often be located near to a limestone quarry.

2) In the past <u>ports</u> were important because they were the source of any <u>imported</u> raw materials. Good examples are Liverpool and Bristol.

Labour Supply has influenced Industrial Location

1) <u>The availability of labour supply</u> is important to industry. A new factory is likely to locate where there are enough people looking for work to fill their needs. Unemployment levels vary enormously by region, so this can be an important factor.

2) The labour supply must be <u>suitable</u>, i.e. there must be enough people who have the <u>right skills</u> to do the job.

Transport influences location in Two Ways

1) The <u>cost of transporting</u> raw materials and the finished product:
If the <u>raw materials</u> cost <u>more</u> to transport than the finished product (they may produce a lot of waste during manufacture, for instance) it is cheaper to locate <u>near the raw materials</u>. If the <u>finished product</u> is <u>more</u> expensive to transport (it may take up more space, or be expensive to insure) then the cheaper location will be <u>nearer the market</u>, e.g. car manufacturing.

2) The <u>type of transport</u> used:
Traditionally, bulky cargo was transported by <u>rail</u>, so rail links were important. The increase in <u>road transport</u> in recent years has changed this. Location near <u>main trunk roads</u>, particularly motorway intersections, has become <u>vital</u> for many industries. <u>Small high-value items</u> can be transported by <u>air</u>, but this is <u>expensive</u>. Goods destined for <u>overseas markets</u> are transported by <u>ship</u>, often using container lorries and roll-on roll-off ferries.

The Market influences industrial location

1) <u>The market</u> is where a product is <u>sold</u> — usually a lot of separate places.

2) Location <u>near</u> the market is best when <u>transporting</u> the product is <u>expensive</u>. For some UK industries who export to Europe, a location in southern England has become attractive.

3) When products are <u>sent on</u> from one industry to another it helps to be located <u>close by</u>. This leads to <u>industrial agglomeration</u> — a concentration of <u>linked industry</u> in one area.

Remember — these are patterns in industry, not hard and fast rules

I know it's not entirely thrilling stuff but you really do need to know it well. Don't forget — real bosses <u>aren't</u> always rational in choosing locations. Sometimes they just like a place.

Changing Industry in the UK

The importance of different types of industries changes over time.

Traditional Manufacturing has Declined and the Service Sector has Grown

1) Raw Materials have started to Run Out

Many <u>natural resources</u> have been <u>used up</u> (see page 105) and others are <u>too expensive</u> to continue extracting, e.g. mining tin in Cornwall is now too expensive. Some materials are now <u>imported</u> from abroad.

2) Competition from other countries has Increased

Many countries, especially <u>LEDCs</u>, manufacture goods at <u>cheaper costs</u> than we can. This is often due to <u>lower wages</u> and <u>worse working conditions</u>, as well as <u>less strict</u> pollution controls.

This has Two Effects on industrial location

1) Many industries have <u>relocated near ports</u> which are now the <u>source</u> of raw materials (for example oil refining, iron and steel in South Wales). Many industries have moved south.

2) New industries are often <u>footloose</u>, meaning they are <u>not</u> tied to a raw material location, and locate in pleasant environments <u>near transport routes</u> and <u>near the markets</u> (e.g. hi-tech industries like computing).

Not too much to learn, but don't miss any of it out

The relationship between raw materials and industry has changed, and you need to understand the reasons why and describe how this has affected modern industry.

Changing Industry in the UK

The **Service Sector** is now the **Largest Employer** in MEDCs

Increases in <u>tertiary industries</u> like finance, insurance, healthcare etc. mean that <u>manufacturing</u> employs a smaller proportion of the working population.

The pie charts show the change:

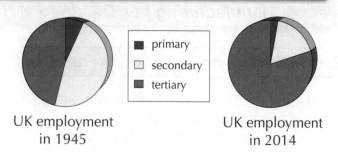

UK employment in 1945   UK employment in 2014

primary
secondary
tertiary

The **Government** affects industry in the UK

The British government is trying to change industry in <u>four ways</u>:

1) Setting up <u>industrial areas</u> (trading estates) and <u>Enterprise Zones</u> to encourage new industrial and commercial businesses.

2) Encouraging companies to set up where there's <u>high unemployment</u> by giving <u>incentives</u> like cheap rent.

3) Encouraging the development of <u>derelict</u> areas, e.g. Docklands of London.

4) Encouraging <u>foreign investment</u> into the UK.

Footloose Industries often locate in science parks

<u>Science parks</u> (e.g. Cambridge Science Park) are estates of modern, usually footloose industries such as pharmaceuticals (medicines) and computing, which have grown up in recent years on the outskirts of towns.

There are three main reasons for their growth:

1) The need to be near <u>raw material</u> has been replaced by the need to be near <u>research centres</u> like universities and similar industries. Developments in hi-tech industry happen so fast that companies need to stay up-to-date to survive.

2) Land is often <u>cheaper</u> on the <u>town outskirts</u> than in the traditional central industrial areas, and access to transport routes is better.

3) <u>Information technology</u> is increasingly allowing hi-tech industry to locate further away from heavily populated areas — for example 'Silicon Glen' in Scotland.

Tertiary industry is now the biggest industrial sector in the UK

Make sure you know why <u>traditional</u> industry has declined and <u>footloose industries</u> and the <u>service sector</u> have grown. And watch the news for <u>up-to-date case studies</u>.

The Use and Abuse of Resources

The world's resources are in greater demand nowadays, and some of them are running low.

The World's Resources are being used up Quicker Than Ever

1) Economic activities use up natural resources, e.g. primary industries like fishing reduce fish stocks, and tertiary businesses use electricity which has been generated through burning fossil fuels.

2) The world's population is increasing so more resources are being used up to meet the needs of more people.

3) Standards of living are increasing for more people as countries become more developed. Higher standards of living mean using more goods and services, so more natural resources are consumed.

4) Some resources are running out, e.g. there's only a limited supply of oil and gas and some species of fish may die out if we catch too many.

5) Use of resources can be managed sustainably so that they don't run out, or so that they last for longer...

Sustainable resource use means looking after Future Generations

> Sustainable use of resources means using resources in a way that lets people living now have the things they need, but without reducing the ability of people in the future to meet their needs.

Some resources like wood are RENEWABLE — they won't run out, provided we plant trees to replace those that are used. But other natural resources are NON-RENEWABLE — they take thousands of years to form and we only have a limited supply of them, e.g. coal, oil and gas.

We can help make sure our use of renewable and non-renewable resources affects future generations as little as possible by:

1) RESOURCE CONSERVATION — Using resources carefully to slow our consumption of them, e.g. making cars and power stations more efficient so less fuel is used.

2) RESOURCE SUBSTITUTION — Changing resources for more sustainable ones, e.g. using easily recyclable card instead of plastic film for packaging products, or using wind power instead of coal.

3) POLLUTION CONTROL — Limiting pollution to reduce problems like global warming and acid rain.

4) RECYCLING — Used to reduce the amount of waste produced and as part of resource conservation.

A growing population needs more resources

We can all look after future generations by reducing demand for resources, recycling more and switching to renewable resources where we can. Your grandchildren will thank you...

Energy and Power

The energy we need comes from <u>natural resources</u>, and is converted into power supplies at <u>power stations</u> — usually in the form of <u>electricity</u> or <u>gas</u>.

Most of our Energy Resources are Non-Renewable

<u>FOSSIL FUELS</u> (oil, coal and gas) are <u>non-renewable</u> resources. They have traditionally supplied most of our energy, but they are <u>not</u> sustainable and are a major source of <u>pollution</u>.

Renewable Sources of energy are improving

As <u>fossil fuels</u> have started to run out, <u>alternative</u> sources of energy have been suggested.

Things like <u>running water</u>, the <u>wind</u> and the <u>Sun</u> are renewable and can be used to generate power. They are <u>sustainable sources</u> that don't cause as much pollution.

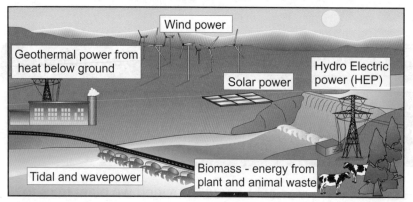

Wind power

Geothermal power from heat below ground

Solar power

Hydro Electric power (HEP)

Tidal and wavepower

Biomass - energy from plant and animal waste

These energy sources won't run out, but at the moment there are <u>two</u> big problems with their use:

1) <u>Alternative energy sources</u> can't produce as much power as fossil fuel power stations without being gigantic.

2) They can be <u>very expensive</u>.

There are Three Major Issues in the Energy Debate

1) Balancing	the need for <u>power</u> and the need to <u>protect</u> the <u>environment</u> from pollution.
2) Technology	must be developed to help <u>find</u> and <u>improve</u> use of <u>alternative energy sources</u>.
3) Energy use	in general must become more <u>efficient</u>, so that less energy is wasted.

See pages 118-120 for more on pollution caused by fossil fuels.

The essential point: fossil fuels will eventually run out

Make sure you know the <u>facts</u> about fossil fuels and alternative energy sources. Then you've got to get the <u>issues</u> straight as well. Everybody has different <u>views</u> on power production and its effect on the environment but you need to know <u>all sides</u> of the debate.

Fishing and Mining

Fishing and mining are two primary industries that can be <u>unsustainable</u> if not managed properly.

Fish Stocks are being Used Up

Fishing is a huge industry, but we have to take care to avoid catching fish (e.g. cod) <u>unsustainably</u>.

Overfishing can also disrupt food chains — see pages 116-117.

1) <u>Overfishing</u> (catching fish more quickly than they can reproduce) is <u>depleting</u> fish resources. For example, stocks of <u>bluefin tuna</u> in the northern Pacific Ocean have <u>decreased</u> by <u>96%</u> due to overfishing.

2) Fishing boats also kill aquatic animals by <u>leaking oil</u> and <u>diesel</u> into the sea.

3) <u>Quotas</u> (limits on the number of fish caught) can be introduced to stop overfishing — but these are <u>hard to enforce</u> and can lead to fish catches being <u>thrown back</u> to avoid breaking the quota.

4) Fish can be raised on <u>fish farms</u> to prevent wild stocks from running out — but fish farms can cause <u>pollution</u> and some people think it's <u>cruel</u> to keep fish in farms.

Managing Mining of resources is a Balancing Act

1) Many <u>really useful</u> resources are extracted by <u>mining</u>. For example, coal used in power stations, metals used in cars and stone used in house building are all extracted from mines.

2) Mines <u>use up</u> the natural resources in an area, then leave the environment <u>damaged</u>.

3) Most types of mining use lots of <u>water</u>, so mining can also <u>deplete</u> water resources.

4) Some kinds of mining can cause <u>air</u>, <u>water</u> or <u>noise pollution</u>.

5) Mining can be made more sustainable by introducing <u>laws</u> to help <u>reduce pollution</u>, or by <u>restoring plants</u> in areas that are no longer an active part of the mine.

6) It can be <u>challenging</u> for countries to manage mines so that they can produce <u>affordable raw materials</u>, without causing too much <u>damage to the environment</u>.

Finding ways to deal with the resource problem can be costly

The tough thing about this topic is making sure you can fit it all together. All you really need to know is <u>what</u> resources are, how they're <u>abused</u> and the difficulties of <u>managing</u> them.

SECTION EIGHT — ECONOMIC ACTIVITY AND THE USE OF NATURAL RESOURCES

Deforestation and Conservation

Forests are a natural resource. Cutting down forests is called deforestation. These two pages try to explain why deforestation occurs, and why some people think it's a bad thing.

In **Brazil** trees are disappearing for **Five** reasons

1) Trees are logged and exported to MEDCs. For the logging industry to keep doing this in the long-term they need to replace the trees they remove. However, many LEDCs don't plant for the future because they are more concerned with making money today.

2) The population is increasing and the government wants to build settlements and roads in the tropical rainforest. Tress have to be cut down to make space.

3) The forest is cleared to set up cattle ranches which quickly make the land useless.

4) Mineral extraction helps Brazil pay foreign debts — Carajas is the world's largest iron reserve. Forest is removed to make way for roads and mines.

5) Hydro-electric power (HEP) development has meant that large areas of land have been flooded.

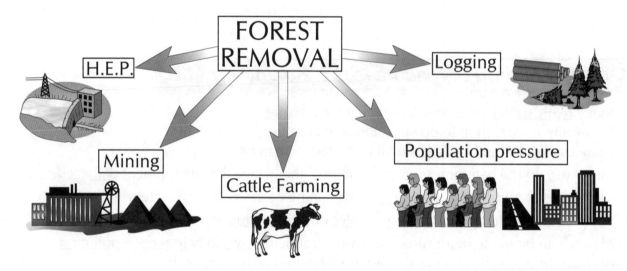

Western Siberia has a deforestation problem

Since 1970, Western Siberia has produced oil and natural gas. Coniferous forests were felled to pave the way for exploration. Oil spills have polluted water and land, and there have been fires. It's feared the ecosystem won't recover — plants take ages to re-establish in such a severe climate.

See p.116-117 for more on ecosystems.

There are many reasons for deforestation

Both in Brazil and in Western Siberia industrial and financial pressures mean that trees are cut down to make way for other things. Preserving forest is the best option but it would be very costly.

Deforestation and Conservation

Two sides to the **Deforestation Debate**

For Conservation

1) <u>Agricultural development</u> is pointless — <u>soils</u> robbed of tropical rainforest <u>lose fertility</u>, so farming can't continue after three or four years.

2) <u>Medicinal products</u> could be <u>destroyed</u> before they're discovered or researched — medicines have been found here before.

3) <u>Heritage value</u> means <u>preserving</u> this ecosystem for future generations — there are many <u>native tribes</u> whose way of life is being destroyed.

4) <u>Global warming</u> is <u>reduced</u> by rainforests because the trees and plants use up <u>carbon dioxide</u> in photosynthesis. High levels of carbon dioxide cause global warming — so removing the forest means more global warming.

5) Forest removal alters the <u>climate</u>. Ethiopia was 40% forest in the early 1900s but is now only 4.6%, causing <u>drought</u> as rainfall has been reduced.

For Deforestation

1) <u>Poverty</u> means a country needs to use <u>all resources</u> to help its people.

2) Many <u>MEDCs</u> destroyed their own forests when <u>developing</u> — the UK did (although not so fast) — so they shouldn't have one rule for themselves and one for <u>LEDCs</u> who need to develop.

3) Most <u>world carbon dioxide emission</u> comes from <u>MEDCs</u> — why should LEDCs have to change policy first?

4) If <u>LEDCs</u> are removing forest to earn <u>money</u> to pay MEDCs, then MEDCs could <u>lower interest</u> or <u>cancel debts</u> if they're so worried about deforestation.

5) <u>MEDCs</u> are buying the <u>products</u> of these areas — so why should LEDCs stop?

Deforestation is not a clear cut issue

There you are then — the great deforestation debate. Remember that whatever you may think, you still need to know <u>both</u> sides of the argument.

Sustainable Development in Forests

There are ways to <u>log trees sustainably</u> and to <u>discourage bad forestry practice</u>.

The world's forests are **Disappearing** fast

1) Forests all over the world are being destroyed for wood, redevelopment, fossil fuels, and farming. <u>Thirteen million</u> hectares of the world's tropical forests disappear <u>every year</u> (1 hectare — 10 000m^2). That's an area approximately the size of Greece lost every year, and it's getting <u>worse</u>.

2) This stuff has been known about for a long time. The problem is getting people to change their use of forests when it usually means making <u>less money</u> in the short-term.

The **Four** big **Sustainable** forestry techniques

<u>CABLING</u>: Most forestry is done by <u>clear cutting</u> which is just ploughing into the forest, cutting down lots of trees you don't want, to get to the ones you do. <u>Cabling</u> is where you pull the trees out using cables and winches, <u>reducing</u> the amount of <u>damage</u> done to the forest.

<u>REPLANTING</u>: Replacing trees that are cut down. More and more <u>laws</u> insist that logging companies do this nowadays. It's important that the right <u>kinds</u> of trees are planted — planting rubber trees instead of lots of different rainforest species isn't good enough.

<u>ZONING</u>: Identifying areas (or zones) for different uses. Different areas are set aside for things like tourism, forestry and mining. Some zones are set up as <u>national parks</u> to protect the forest <u>ecosystem</u>.

<u>SELECTIVE LOGGING</u>: This is a method used by small, <u>environmentally sound</u> logging businesses. Only <u>selected trees</u> are chopped — most trees are left standing. Some of the best trees are left standing to maintain a strong <u>gene pool</u>. The least intrusive form is '<u>horse logging</u>' — dragging felled trees out of the forest using horses instead of huge trucks.

There's a **Three** pronged attack on **Bad** forestry

Promoting sustainable use of the forests

1) Creating a <u>demand</u> for sustainable products. <u>Clearly labelling</u> products from '<u>sustainably managed forests</u>'.

2) Encouraging <u>small-scale projects</u> — e.g. The Body Shop® buying henna (a product used in hair dyes) from forest communities to give them another source of income.

3) Encouraging <u>ecotourism</u> (sustainable tourism that has less impact on the environment) by advertising and education.

Discouraging bad practice

1) <u>Banning</u> wood from forests that are managed non-sustainably.

2) <u>Preventing</u> illegal logging and creating protected areas.

3) Put <u>pressure</u> on businesses to only buy from sustainable forests.

Reducing the need for large-scale deforestation

<u>DEBT-FOR-NATURE SWAPS</u> — some of a country's debt can be bought back by governments or conservation organisations in return for increased commitment to conservation projects.

Water Demand and Supply

Rivers are <u>vital</u> to people. We use water for farming, industry, cooking, washing, toilets and most importantly drinking.

Water companies manage the *water supply*

1) <u>UK water companies</u> are all based on <u>major drainage basins</u> and they try to <u>balance</u> the water <u>supply</u> with the water <u>demand</u>.

2) They control water processing plants and monitor rivers and lakes. They are in charge of things like making sure the water is safe to drink and building and maintaining dams.

The **Environment Agency** monitors the water companies

The water companies are regulated by the <u>Environment Agency</u> in England and Wales and by the <u>Scottish Environment Protection Agency</u> (SEPA) in Scotland.

> The Environment Agency makes sure water companies are doing things <u>safely</u> and <u>sustainably</u>.

Water Demand is *Growing* all the time

1) Until recently, people in the <u>UK</u> have taken a clean, adequate water supply for <u>granted</u>.

2) More <u>demand</u> now means <u>shortages</u> — so people have to help <u>save water</u>:

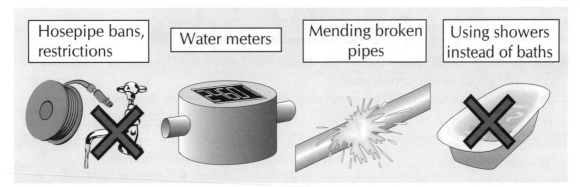

| Hosepipe bans, restrictions | Water meters | Mending broken pipes | Using showers instead of baths |

3) The problem in Britain is that rainfall is <u>heaviest</u> in the north and west but there are more <u>people</u> and <u>industries</u> in the drier south and east.

4) The supply <u>doesn't</u> meet demand — rain is <u>heavier</u> in winter, demand is <u>higher</u> in summer.

5) <u>Storage</u> and <u>movement of water</u> is important but <u>expensive</u>, and <u>quality</u> must be <u>controlled</u>.

The water supply in Britain no longer meets demand

Water supply is a <u>serious</u> issue nowadays at home and abroad. Have another good look at this page and check you know what people can do to save water.

112

Water Demand and Supply

Water supply isn't just an issue in Britain, it's a problem all over the world.

Many **LEDCs** have serious **Water Supply Problems**

1) In 2010, 783 million people had <u>no clean water supply</u> — 11% of the world population.
2) <u>Sanitation</u> is <u>limited</u> to only 64% of the world's people — the rest do without!
3) This is a major <u>health hazard</u> — lack of clean water and sanitation causes 88% of diseases in LEDCs.
4) <u>Demand</u> for water is also <u>increasing</u> as the countries develop and populations grow.
5) <u>Rainfall supplies</u> can often be <u>unreliable</u> and <u>limited</u> in LEDCs — especially hot countries. In the worst cases, <u>droughts</u> can ruin crops and leave thousands without enough clean water. E.g. east Africa, 2011.

LEDCs can **Improve** the water situation

1) Farmers can use <u>sprays</u> or '<u>drip-feeding</u>' to water their crops so no water is <u>wasted</u>.
2) <u>Self-help schemes</u> can enable people to build <u>simple wells</u>.
3) <u>Concrete lining</u> of wells can <u>reduce water loss</u> through evaporation and seepage.
4) <u>Educating</u> people about <u>clean water</u> and <u>sanitation</u> is also very important.

The water situation in **Egypt** — a real case study

The <u>Aswan Dam</u> on the <u>Nile</u> was built in the upper reaches of the river in the 1960s to try to solve some of Egypt's water problems.

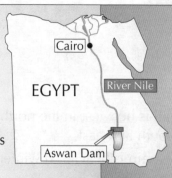

ADVANTAGES
1) Steady water levels.
2) Flood control is possible.
3) Higher crop yields.
4) River can be used for transport all year.
5) Hydro-electric power schemes provide power to help economic development.

DISADVANTAGES
1) More Bilharzia snails that cause disease in humans.
2) Less sediment washed onto flood plains — more fertiliser needed.
3) Dam expensive to build.
4) Hot country — high water loss due to high evaporation rates.
5) Sediment will eventually fill reservoir.

Remember — the water has to be clean

Some places might have loads of water, but if it isn't clean it can't be used. There's no easy way to manage water supply — look at the Aswan Dam for example.

Questions

Phew! There's loads packed into this section — ease yourself in with the warm-up questions.

Warm-up Questions

1) Write a definition of the four types of industry, and give two examples of each.

2) Place the following jobs under the correct heading: primary, secondary, tertiary or quaternary. Nurse, electrician, farmer, research scientist, fisherman, violin-maker, double-glazing salesman, car factory worker, coal miner, librarian, forestry worker, solicitor, taxi driver.

3) Why do ports have an important influence on industrial location?

4) What are 'non-renewable' resources?

5) Give one advantage and one disadvantage of mining.

6) Give two ways that people in MEDCs can save water.

7) Give three advantages and three disadvantages of the Aswan Dam.

Practice Questions

Make sure you understand the basic themes of each topic then have a go at these questions.

1) The grid below describes the four types of industry. Copy it and fill in the blanks.

Type of industry	What it involves	Example 1	Example 2
Primary			
	Manufacturing a product	House building	
Tertiary		Advertising	
	Research and development		Crop research

2) All the companies below were involved in making a book and getting it to the bookshop.

The New Zealand Forestry Company	The PaperMakery *Finest quality paper*	Harvey & Daughter Manufacturers of books since 1950
TZC Laboratories Tree & plant genetics	Baffin & Braithwaite BOOKSHOP	Kutter & Company Logger

a) Which two companies are primary industries?

b) Which company provides a tertiary service directly to the public?

c) Write down the steps involved in converting tree seedlings into the books we buy.

d) Is this statement true or false? 'TZC laboratories are a secondary manufacturer'.

SECTION EIGHT — ECONOMIC ACTIVITY AND THE USE OF NATURAL RESOURCES

Questions

3)   Answer the following questions:

a)   What does using resources sustainably mean?

b)   Copy and complete these four key things that sustainable resource use involves:

i)   R_____ conservation

ii)   Resource s_____.

iii)   P_____ control.

iv)   Recycling to reduce the amount of w_____ produced.

4)   Copy and complete the following description of
energy production using the words supplied below.

gas   natural resources   coal   power stations   electricity

Energy is obtained from _____ like

_____ or_____, which are

converted to _____ at _____.

5)   There are arguments both for and against deforestation. Write two lists, one <u>for</u>
deforestation and one <u>against</u>, putting each of the following points into the correct list.

a)   More than half of all medicines were originally discovered in trees and plants in forests.

b)   Many LEDCs' economies rely on exporting timber from forests.

c)   Many native tribes live in forests.

d)   Firewood is essential in many LEDCs.

e)   Removing forests reduces rainfall, causing drought.

f)   Trees absorb carbon dioxide and so help to reduce global warming.

g)   Most of the nutrients in a tropical rainforest are in the trees and not in the soil.

h)   Wildlife habitats should be preserved to maintain biodiversity (a wide variety of
plants and animals).

i)   MEDCs such as the UK deforested large areas when they were developing.

6)   List two ways of discouraging bad practice in forestry.

Section Eight — Summary Questions

There's a lot of stuff in here — industry, use and abuse of resources, energy, deforestation and water demand. You won't really know if you know it or not until you test yourself and that's where these questions come in. They're not easy so don't expect to whizz through them first time round. Work your way through them all — if you get stuck, go back and learn the problem topic. Don't just finish with the questions when you can do them all — they're useful to come back to later on to see if you've forgotten 'owt.

1) What is a primary industry?

2) What kind of industry is a tyre factory?

3) Give two examples of tertiary industries.

4) What are the four big influences on the location of industry?

5) Give two ways in which labour supply can influence the location of industry.

6) What is a 'footloose' industry?

7) Explain the four ways that the British government is trying to change industry in the UK.

8) What two factors are increasing to cause a bigger demand on resources?

9) What does 'sustainable use of resources' mean?

10) What is the key difference between renewable and non-renewable resources?

11) Name three renewable resources we can use to make electricity.

12) What are the three major issues in the energy debate?

13) Give two ways fishing can be made more sustainable to help prevent overfishing.

14) Name three resources we get from mining.

15) Give five main reasons why tropical rainforests are being removed in Brazil.

16) Explain the reason why deforestation has occurred in Siberia.

17) Give three arguments used by conservationists against deforestation.

18) How can forest removal affect: a) local rainfall,   b) global warming?

19) How could MEDCs help to discourage deforestation?

20) How much of the world's forest disappears every year?

21) Describe the three ways that bad forestry is being attacked.

22) Name two ways in which people in the UK can help to save water.

23) How can LEDCs reduce their demand for water?

Ecosystem Cycles and the Human Effect

Ecosystems are made up of linked parts which all depend on each other — if one part goes wrong, the whole ecosystem will break down.

A Food Chain is a series of Links in an Ecosystem

1) Most food chains start with green plants which are called primary producers as they use the sun's energy to photosynthesise, i.e. make their food. This is the word equation for photosynthesis:

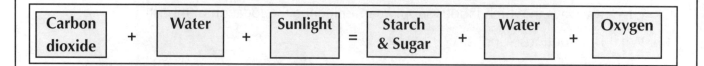

Carbon dioxide	+	Water	+	Sunlight	=	Starch & Sugar	+	Water	+	Oxygen

2) Some animals known as herbivores eat these plants, e.g. cows eat grass.

3) Other animals known as carnivores eat the herbivores, e.g. humans eat cows.

4) Organisms die and nutrients return to the soil when bacteria and fungi decompose the dead material making it ready for re-use. This means the process goes in a cycle.

primary producer   herbivore   carnivore

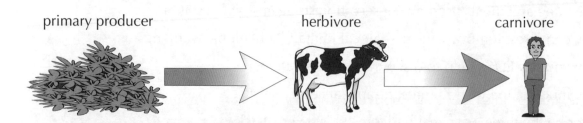

5) Humans depend on food chains for lots of things, e.g. food and medicines.

6) But humans can disrupt food chains by destroying habitats, through climate change or by over-exploiting one part of the chain.

Nice and easy — and lots of clear diagrams for you to copy out

Learn how the food chain works. Try thinking of your own examples of food chains, scribble them down, then label the primary producers, herbivores and carnivores.

Ecosystem Cycles and the Human Effect

There are **Two Main Cycles** in an ecosystem

1) The carbon cycle: Carbon is released by burning things that contain carbon (e.g. fossil fuels) and by respiration (we breathe out carbon dioxide). This carbon dioxide (CO_2) is then absorbed by plants — they convert it into sugars using photosynthesis. We then eat the plants or burn them, releasing the carbon dioxide for the plants to use again.

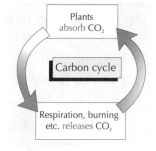

2) The nitrogen cycle: There are nitrates (a form of nitrogen) in the soil. Plants absorb these nitrates and use them to make proteins. Animals eat the plants. Animals excrete the nitrogen as ammonia, which is broken down by bacteria into nitrates. The nitrates soak into the soil ready for the plants to use them again.

3) Humans can affect both these cycles. Huge amounts of CO_2 are released by burning fossil fuels, while deforestation reduces the amount of CO_2 that can be absorbed. Adding fertiliser to soil can alter the nitrogen cycle too and can cause environmental problems like algal blooms.

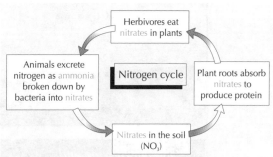

Many **Ecosystems** are affected by **People**

1) In the UK, much of our natural forest has been removed to make way for farming and for building towns and cities.

2) In North America, many areas of natural grassland have been removed to grow cereal crops. Some were regularly burned by Native American Indians in the past to stop tree growth on the land they wanted to use for grazing.

3) If land is left alone it will develop into a natural climax community (where the natural vegetation has developed fully). In the UK, this climax community is normally deciduous woodland, e.g. oak woodland. There are many areas in the world where human activity prevents an ecosystem developing fully. If the land is farmed or used for grazing, it stops this natural development and the land stays the same.

- From 1945 to 1985 Nepal, in the Himalayas, removed half its forests to give land for farming to the growing population. Because it is a mountainous country, this caused large-scale soil erosion. Material was washed into the River Ganges, which starts in the Nepalese mountains and runs through India and then through Bangladesh.

- The depth of the river Ganges' bed was reduced by the soil that had been washed down. This increased flooding risks in the delta area in Bangladesh.

There are several ways that people can affect their environment

The important thing to remember here is that people can have a dramatic effect on the natural environment they live in. Deforestation in Nepal is a good example.

Acid Rain

Acid rain is rain which has a <u>higher acid level</u> than normal (it has a low pH).
It's another way that humans can affect the environment.

Acid Rain comes from Burning Fossil Fuels

1) <u>Burning</u> coal, oil and natural gas in power stations gives off <u>sulphur dioxide gas</u>.

2) <u>Burning</u> petrol and oil in vehicle engines gives off <u>nitrogen oxides</u> as gases.

3) These gases <u>mix</u> with <u>water vapour</u> and <u>rain water</u> in the atmosphere, producing weak solutions of <u>sulphuric</u> and <u>nitric acids</u> — which fall as acid rain.

$SO_2 + NO_x$ ⇒ ⇒ + Clean Cloud = Acid Cloud ⇒ Acid Rain

| Sulphur dioxide and nitrogen oxides | + | Water vapour | ⇒ | Acid rain |

Acid rain Damages Nature and Buildings

1) <u>Leaves</u> and <u>tree roots</u> can <u>die</u> from the poisonous rain.

2) <u>High acid levels</u> make rivers and lakes unsuitable for <u>fish</u>.

3) Acid rain increases 'leaching' which removes <u>nutrients</u> from <u>soils</u> — crop yields <u>decrease</u>.

4) Acid rain <u>dissolves</u> the stonework and mortar of <u>buildings</u>, e.g. York Minster has a lot of crumbling stonework.

5) Often acid rain <u>doesn't</u> fall where the gases are <u>produced</u> — high chimneys <u>disperse</u> the gases and winds blow them <u>great distances</u> before they <u>dissolve</u> and <u>fall to Earth</u> as rain. E.g. gases produced in England and western Europe can result in acid rainfall in Scotland and Scandinavia.

Acid rain Production can be Reduced

1) <u>Sulphur dioxide</u> can be <u>removed</u> from power station chimneys but this process is expensive.

2) <u>Less sulphur dioxide</u> will be produced if the <u>demand</u> for electricity is <u>reduced</u>, or if it's generated using <u>other production methods</u>.

3) Fitting <u>catalytic converters</u> to vehicle exhausts <u>removes</u> the <u>oxides of nitrogen</u>.

4) <u>Limiting</u> the number of <u>road vehicles</u> and increasing <u>public transport</u> would cut down on exhaust gas emissions.

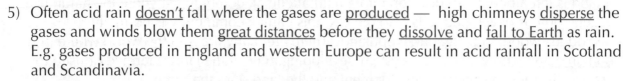

The gases can travel a long distance before they fall as acid rain

Make sure you understand the acid rain equation. Try writing a few sentences describing how acid rain is created, what effects it has and how it can be reduced.

Global Warming

The <u>average global temperature</u> has <u>risen</u> by 0.85 °C in the last hundred years — and the years since 1980 have been the hottest on record.

There's more on climate changes on page 37.

Global Warming is caused by increased Fossil Fuel Use

1) Since the <u>industrial revolution</u>, people have needed <u>more energy</u> for work and in the home — this has come from burning <u>more fossil fuels</u>, particularly coal and oil.

2) This <u>burning</u> releases more <u>carbon dioxide</u> and <u>methane</u> (greenhouse gases) into the atmosphere — these contribute to what's known as '<u>the greenhouse effect</u>'.

Earth is like a giant Greenhouse

<u>Energy</u> from the <u>Sun</u> passes through the <u>atmosphere</u> as light and <u>warms up the Earth</u>. When the energy is radiated and <u>reflected</u> back off the surface as <u>heat</u>, it is <u>trapped</u> by the atmosphere and <u>can't get back out</u> into space — this is how a <u>greenhouse</u> keeps the heat inside. Increasing the greenhouse gases increases the greenhouse effect, which means the Earth gets <u>hotter</u>.

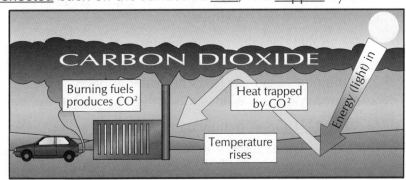

CARBON DIOXIDE

Burning fuels produces CO²

Heat trapped by CO²

Temperature rises

Energy (light) in

Global warming causes Sea Levels to Rise

1) <u>Ice-sheets</u> and <u>glaciers</u> are beginning to <u>melt</u>.

2) <u>Sea levels</u> have <u>risen</u> by <u>10 - 20 cm</u> in the <u>last 100 years</u>.

3) <u>In 100 years</u>, sea levels will probably rise <u>another 0.8 - 2 m</u>.

4) <u>Low-lying areas</u> of the world are under threat of <u>flooding</u> — e.g. parts of south east England, the Nile and Ganges deltas and most major world cities.

5) Global warming also causes <u>freak weather</u>, e.g storms and droughts, and might change the world's climate, e.g. the Sahara could spread north into Europe and the tundra could become warm enough to grow crops.

Greenhouse Gases need to be Reduced

1) <u>Britain</u> and <u>Europe</u> have agreed to <u>reduce</u> gas emissions — they're big users of fossil fuels.

2) Some <u>LEDCs</u> don't want to because their <u>rate of development</u> would <u>slow down</u>.

3) <u>Oil states</u> in the Gulf don't want to because their <u>revenues</u> from <u>oil sales</u> would <u>go down</u>.

4) Some <u>MEDCs</u> don't want to because they don't want a fall in <u>living standards</u>.

Remember the chemicals and fuels involved in this process

The energy we create by burning fossil fuels creates gases that form a layer around the Earth. This traps heat around the Earth's surface, causing flooding, and a host of other problems...

Pollution

Pollution is any damage caused to the environment — humans cause a lot of pollution.

Pollution is a Global Problem

1) It's found worldwide — pollution created in one part of the world can affect others, e.g. radioactive fallout from the Chernobyl disaster affected north-west England.

2) Industry, transport and agriculture can cause pollution — almost any human activity can. Ugly buildings, tips and quarries cause visual pollution, and aircraft cause noise pollution.

There are Four common Types of Pollution

1) AIR POLLUTION is created by burning fossil fuels for industrial, domestic and transport use — giving off gases like sulphur dioxide and carbon monoxide, smoke, small particles and droplets. Agricultural chemicals also get into the air.

2) RIVER POLLUTION comes from untreated industrial waste and dirty water. Fertilisers and pesticides from agriculture also get washed into water courses. Hot water from power stations causes thermal pollution.

3) SEA POLLUTION is mainly caused by dirty water from industry, oil slicks and spills, and untreated human sewage. Household waste is sometimes dumped in the sea.

4) LAND POLLUTION comes from agricultural chemicals, waste material from mines and quarries, scrap, industrial waste and household waste.

Pollution has serious Harmful Effects

1) Air pollution causes acid rain, increases the greenhouse effect, and is linked to illnesses like asthma.

2) Water pollution can poison the water supply and destroy river habitats — e.g. untreated sewage spreads diseases.

3) Land pollution can kill wildlife — e.g. insecticides kill insects.

4) Many pollutants stay around for years — they get into animal and human food chains, e.g. people died in Minamata Bay, Japan, because they ate fish contaminated by industrial mercury waste.

5) Some chemical waste products from industry are toxic — e.g. asbestos (used as an insulator) gives off dust which causes cancer.

6) Radioactive waste from nuclear power takes ages to biodegrade. High level waste causes cancer and genetic defects in most life forms.

Four common types of pollution to learn — turn it all into bullet points

This is pretty gruesome stuff, but you've got to learn it. Don't forget that pollution is a global problem and it can only be solved on a global scale.

Farming and Soil Erosion

All farming <u>affects</u> the <u>environment</u> to some extent.

Farming can cause Soil Erosion

1) <u>Soil erosion</u> is a problem in <u>LEDCs</u> (e.g. erosion by water in Nepal) and <u>MEDCs</u> (erosion by wind in Oklahoma) and is associated with <u>misuse</u> of the environment, often by <u>farming techniques</u>. It's a major problem because soil takes <u>hundreds of years</u> to form, and once removed, is <u>very difficult</u> to replace.

2) The two agents of soil erosion are <u>wind</u> and <u>water</u>. Once soil is left bare, it is <u>vulnerable</u> to being either <u>blown</u> or <u>washed away</u>. These are the ways it can happen:

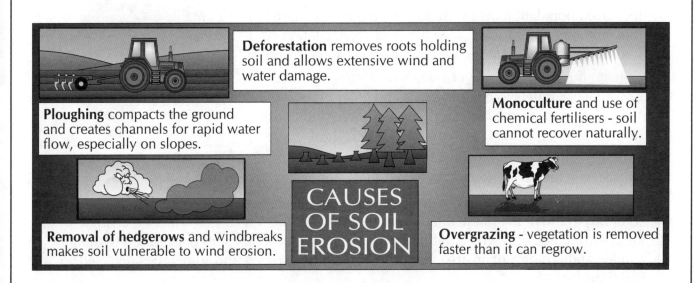

Deforestation removes roots holding soil and allows extensive wind and water damage.

Ploughing compacts the ground and creates channels for rapid water flow, especially on slopes.

Monoculture and use of chemical fertilisers - soil cannot recover naturally.

Removal of hedgerows and windbreaks makes soil vulnerable to wind erosion.

CAUSES OF SOIL EROSION

Overgrazing - vegetation is removed faster than it can regrow.

*There are **Six Methods** used to **Limit** soil erosion*

The diagram below shows the different ways soil erosion can be <u>limited</u>:

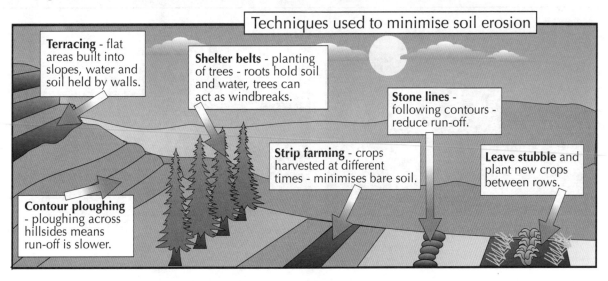

Techniques used to minimise soil erosion

Terracing - flat areas built into slopes, water and soil held by walls.

Shelter belts - planting of trees - roots hold soil and water, trees can act as windbreaks.

Stone lines - following contours - reduce run-off.

Strip farming - crops harvested at different times - minimises bare soil.

Leave stubble and plant new crops between rows.

Contour ploughing - ploughing across hillsides means run-off is slower.

Learn the examples of areas affected by erosion above

Soil erosion is a serious problem for farming and the future of farming. Damage has already been done, and some of the techniques to minimise erosion are costly and time consuming.

Farming and Soil Erosion

Farming causes Desertification

Desertification is when a desert gradually <u>spreads</u> to the surrounding areas of <u>semi-desert</u>, making them <u>true desert</u> (and <u>unsuitable</u> for <u>farming</u>). <u>Human activity</u> is usually one of the main causes of desertification.

*Desertification has **Three Main Causes** and **Few Solutions***

<u>Central Africa</u> is a perfect example of desertification.

Area of severe desertification

Africa

1 Niger   4 Ethiopia
2 Chad   5 Somalia
3 Sudan

1) <u>Increased population</u> means <u>more trees</u> are cut down for fuel, and <u>larger herds</u> overgraze the land — vegetation is removed and the ground is left bare, causing <u>soil erosion</u>.

2) <u>Climate fluctuations</u> — several years of adequate rainfall encourages farmers to <u>enlarge herds</u> and <u>grow crops</u>. If dry years follow, the land <u>can't support</u> increased herds and <u>soil erosion</u> occurs.

3) <u>Commercial agriculture</u> uses <u>valuable water</u> and pushes subsistence farmers onto marginal land that cannot support farming.

> Solutions to the problem are difficult, as desertification often causes dramatic change to the environment. But with careful management and farming techniques suited to the climate and customs of an area, the problem can be avoided and sometimes reversed. Solutions include:
>
> 1) <u>Minimising soil erosion</u> — terracing, strip farming, stone lines, shelter belts etc.
>
> 2) Using <u>branches</u> (not whole trees) for fuel.
>
> 3) <u>Less intensive</u> use of land — leaving it unused every couple of years to recover.
>
> 4) <u>Planting trees</u> that are good for building materials and fruit.

Deserts can't support crops or herds

Deforestation plays a big part in desertification

Human activity can make land unsuitable for farming

Desertification is a big problem in certain areas, and can pose a real threat to the local standard of living and economy. The Africa example is a good one, make sure you know it.

National Parks

National Parks have been set up in England, Wales and Scotland to <u>protect</u> different <u>wild environments</u> from too much <u>damage</u> by people, and keep them as they are.

National Parks are Protected areas

1) There are <u>15 National Parks</u> in Britain, mostly situated away from large population centres.
2) They are areas of <u>natural beauty</u>, including large areas of mountains and moorland — and they are <u>protected</u> by law for the enjoyment of all members of the public.
3) Some activities may be <u>banned</u> or <u>limited</u> if they cause too much environmental damage.
4) Much of the land is <u>privately owned</u>.
5) They contain many <u>permanent settlements</u> like villages.
6) They are looked after by <u>National Park Authorities</u>.

National Parks

Cairngorms
Loch Lomond and The Trossachs
Northumberland
Lake District
North Yorks Moor
Yorkshire Dales
Peak District
Snowdonia
Norfolk Broads
Pembrokeshire Coast
Brecon Beacons
Exmoor
South Downs
Dartmoor
New Forest

These authorities have Three Jobs

1) The National Park Authorities protect the <u>environment</u> from <u>damage</u> by <u>visitors</u> and <u>residents</u>.
2) They promote the <u>enjoyment</u> and <u>understanding</u> of the parks.
3) They look after the interests of the <u>residents</u>.

Many people come to the parks for outdoor activities and to enjoy their peace and natural beauty — the motorway network allows easy access.

The National Parks — pretty areas of countryside, protected by law

On this page we have the fifteen National Parks and on the next page, all the problems with running them — all ready for you to learn.

National Parks

The **Use** of the parks **Causes Conflict**

1) <u>Planning regulations</u> are very strict, and <u>development</u> is strictly <u>controlled</u>.

2) <u>Industries</u> in the parks can cause problems — e.g. limestone quarrying in the Peak District provides jobs yet it destroys the very landscape that people come to see.

3) <u>Visitors</u> and <u>tourists</u> provide most jobs and income for residents, but cause <u>traffic congestion</u>, <u>pollution</u>, <u>litter</u> and <u>footpath erosion</u>.

4) Visitors can <u>cause damage</u> to <u>farmland</u> and <u>animals</u>, destroying farmers' livelihoods.

> <u>Honey-pot areas</u> are the popular spots that become so <u>overused</u> by tourist visitors that they start to <u>change</u> (e.g. supermarkets and hotels are built to cater for the visitors) and eventually <u>lose</u> the character that made them special — e.g. Bowness-on-Windermere in the Lake District.

Conflicts can be **Resolved** — slowly

1) The <u>National Park Authorities</u> try to resolve these conflicts through public <u>enquiries</u>.

2) <u>Planning</u> and <u>development restrictions</u> can control what goes on — e.g. 'park and ride' schemes have restricted vehicular access to parts of the Peak District National Park.

Honey-pot areas are too popular for their own good

The key point here is how to find a <u>balance</u> between <u>encouraging</u> more tourists and visitors, and <u>stopping</u> them from <u>destroying</u> a protected environment.

Questions

You guessed it... here comes the questions, just to make sure you've learnt everything.

Warm-up Questions

1) What is a 'food chain'?

2) What are the two main cycles in an ecosystem called?

3) Give three ways in which the production of acid rain can be reduced.

4) Explain why global warming is causing the sea level to rise.

5) Why might LEDCs not want to reduce greenhouse gas emissions?

6) Describe the five farming methods that lead to soil erosion.

7) Explain why conflicts often arise in National Parks.

Practice Questions

Here's some nice questions to get you started.

1) a) What is a food chain?

   b) Complete the labels on the simple food chain below.

   P_____ p_____   H_____   C_____

   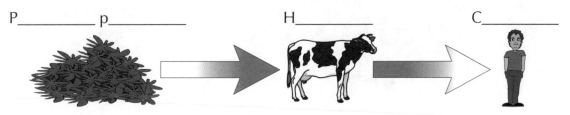

   c) How can humans affect food chains?

2) Copy and complete the following description of
    the carbon cycle using the words supplied below.

   use   carbon   plants   respiration   burning   photosynthesis

   Carbon is released by _____ things that contain _____

   and by _____. This carbon dioxide is then absorbed by

   _____ — they convert it into sugars using _____.

   We then eat the plants or burn them, releasing carbon dioxide for the plants to

   _____ again.

3) Copy and complete the diagram of
    the nitrogen cycle using the labels supplied below.

   Animals excrete nitrogen as ammonia
   broken down by bacteria into nitrates.

   Plant roots absorb nitrates to produce protein.

   Herbivores eat nitrates in plants.

   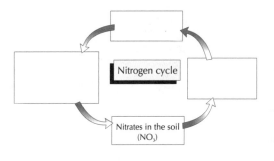

Questions

Now onto acid rain, global warming and soil erosion.

4) Copy and complete this passage by filling in the spaces with the correct words.

Acid rain is a weak solution of _____ and nitric acids.

It forms when chemicals mix with_____ in the atmosphere.

Factories use high _____ to disperse gases, so acid rain may

travel a long _____ before it is deposited.

Chemicals from England can fall in Scotland and Sweden because of the

_____ .

5) Look at the diagram below. Copy and complete the sentences to show the causes of global warming using the words supplied.

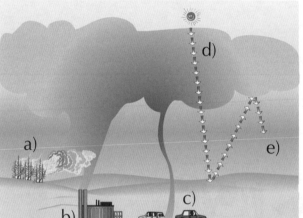

carbon dioxide   fossil fuels   methane

temperature   atmosphere

a) Burning wood as fuel releases the gases _____ _____ and _____ into the air.

b) The burning of _____ _____ releases _____ _____ into the air.

c) Cars burn _____ _____ too.

d) The sun's rays can pass through the _____ and warm the Earth.

e) But heat from the Earth can't escape through the pollution, and so the Earth's _____ rises.

6) Give a brief explanation of each of the methods labelled a - f, which are designed to reduce soil erosion.

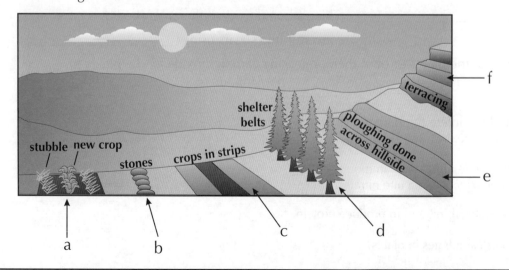

Section Nine — Summary Questions

There's a lot of stuff in here — ecosystems, acid rain, global warming, pollution, farming and soil erosion, and National Parks — they seem like separate topics, but they're not. They're all about how human activity relies on natural systems working well and how human activity can affect these natural systems. Use these questions to test what you do and what you don't know.

1) Is photosynthesis the production of sunlight, food or carbon dioxide?

2) In a food chain, what are animals that eat herbivores known as?

3) Draw a simple diagram of the carbon cycle.

4) Briefly describe what happens in the nitrogen cycle.

5) What is a 'natural climax community'?

6) Explain how acid rain is caused.

7) List two of the damaging effects of acid rain.

8) Why doesn't acid rain always fall in the area where it is produced?

9) Give three ways in which the production of acid rain can be reduced.

10) What causes the greenhouse effect?

11) Use a diagram to explain how the greenhouse effect works.

12) What evidence is there that global warming has taken place in the last hundred years?

13) Explain with an example why pollution is considered to be a global problem.

14) What are the major causes of (a) air pollution and (b) river pollution?

15) Why might a reduction in pollution prove to be unpopular?

16) What is desertification?

17) Name two causes of desertification in Africa.

18) Give two solutions to desertification.

19) Name five of the National Parks in England and Wales.

20) List three of the features of National Parks.

21) Which bodies are responsible for looking after the National Parks?

22) What is a 'honey-pot' area? What problems arise in them?

Nigeria — Physical Geography

Nigeria is an <u>LEDC</u> with many <u>natural resources</u> and different tropical <u>vegetation types</u>.

Nigeria is in Africa

1) Nigeria is a large country in <u>Africa</u> situated just north of the equator. It's about <u>four times larger</u> than the UK.

2) Its physical geography is varied with large areas of <u>tropical rainforest</u>, <u>mangrove</u> and <u>savanna grassland</u>.

3) Nigeria has a huge amount of <u>natural resources</u>, including oil, gas, coal and tin.

Nigeria mostly has a Tropical Climate

1) Nigeria has a tropical climate — its average temperature is <u>27 °C</u> and it gets around <u>1150 mm</u> of <u>precipitation</u> every year (that's quite a lot).

2) Temperatures in the south of Nigeria <u>don't change much</u> throughout the year — winter is only one or two degrees cooler than summer on average.

3) Regions that are further inland tend to have a more <u>arid</u> climate than coastal areas — they are <u>hotter</u> and have <u>less rain</u> (see p.38). This affects the <u>type of plants</u> that can grow...

There are Mangroves and Rainforests near the Coast...

1) Mangroves are <u>collections of trees</u> that are found on <u>tropical coasts</u>. The trees are adapted to live in salty sea water, and they have strong <u>intertwined roots</u> that rise above the sea's surface for support.

2) <u>Rainforests</u> also grow in the tropical climate (see p.4). Some of Nigeria's rainforests have been <u>logged</u> to make way for <u>plantations</u> (e.g. oil palm) and <u>grazing land</u>.

...but Most of Nigeria is Savanna

Areas of savanna grassland (see page 2) have a <u>scattering of trees</u> with <u>grasses</u> below them. Savanna grassland covers the <u>majority</u> of <u>inland</u> Nigeria where precipitation is lower.

The Niger River is the Third Longest River in Africa

The <u>Niger River</u> flows from the northwest corner of Nigeria through to the southern coast, where it joins the Atlantic Ocean at the Niger Delta. It is <u>4200 km long</u>. The <u>Benue River</u> joins the Niger. Both the Benue and the Niger are used to transport goods between Nigeria and its neighbours.

There is a mixture of tropical vegetation types in Nigeria

Although the Niger and Benue rivers provide some water for irrigation, most of Nigeria only receives enough rain for <u>savanna vegetation</u> to grow. Nearer the coast there is more rain, allowing <u>rainforests</u> to grow. Mangroves are found on the shoreline.

Nigeria — Population

Nigeria's population is around <u>177 million</u> — the <u>largest population</u> in <u>Africa</u>, and the 7th largest in the world. That's already pretty big, and it's still <u>growing</u> very <u>quickly</u>.

Nigeria has a **Very High Birth Rate** and a **Lower Death Rate**

1) Nigeria's <u>birth rate</u> is <u>very high</u> — 38 per 1000 people per year. The death rate is also high (13 per 1000 people per year), but not as high as the birth rate.

2) Nigeria is experiencing <u>rapid</u> population growth because of its high birth rate.

3) Nigeria also has a very <u>young population</u> — 43% of the population are under 15 years old.

4) Nigeria's <u>literacy rate</u> is low — only <u>61%</u>. Education also varies by location and gender — in the north, less than a third of young women are literate. *These are all indicators of Nigeria's low level of development.*

The **Population** is **Not Evenly Distributed** across the country

The <u>south</u> of Nigeria is one of the most <u>densely populated areas</u>. There are three main reasons for this:

See page 73 for more on population density

1) Most of the main <u>oil</u> and <u>gas fields</u> are in the south.

2) The south's <u>rainforests</u> are the best areas for growing crops like <u>rubber</u> and <u>cocoa</u>.

3) All the <u>seaports</u>, and most of the <u>industrial centres</u>, are on the Atlantic coast in the south.

Population Growth is **High** in the **Cities**

1) <u>Half</u> of Nigeria's population already live in <u>urban areas</u> (towns and cities).

2) The proportion of the <u>population</u> who live in urban areas is growing rapidly too — many Nigerians have been migrating to cities to look for better job opportunities and education.

3) This has led to many urban areas becoming <u>overcrowded</u>. The cities have grown <u>rapidly without planning</u> — many houses are <u>poor quality</u> and without <u>water</u> or <u>electricity</u> supplies.

4) Many people live in illegal <u>shanty towns</u>, like Makoko in Lagos. The inhabitants don't own the land their houses are built on — this means the homes could be <u>demolished</u> at any time.

5) <u>Unemployment</u> is also high, and many of those who do have jobs are <u>underemployed</u> — they could work more hours or do a job that requires more skills, but there are no such jobs available.

The population is growing rapidly, especially in cities

Nigeria's population is already the <u>largest</u> in <u>Africa</u>, and the growth rate shows no sign of slowing down. This puts a lot of pressure on cities, and on top of all that there is a <u>high</u> rate of <u>migration</u> from rural to urban areas too.

SECTION TEN — A STUDY OF TWO CONTRASTING REGIONS

Nigeria — Farming and Industry

Agriculture and oil have been the most important parts of Nigeria's economy for years.

Nearly Half of Nigerians work in Agriculture

1) About 45% of Nigerians work in agriculture. Most are poor subsistence farmers who have a small amount of land that they use to feed their families. Others work in commercial farming (farming for profit).

2) Agriculture is the largest part of Nigeria's economy — it makes up about 22% of Nigeria's income. The importance of farming has declined though, since the discovery of oil reserves and as the services (e.g. retail, transport) and manufacturing sectors have grown.

3) Nigeria's commercial crops like peanuts, cotton, rubber and palm oil used to make up a lot of Nigeria's exports. Now almost all of Nigeria's exports are oil.

Oil Extraction is a really important industry

1) Extracting crude oil used to dominate Nigeria's economy, but its importance has decreased as other sectors (like transport and financial services) have grown.

2) Most of the oil is exported — oil makes up about 97% of Nigeria's total exports.

3) Oil has to be refined before it can be used. Nigeria doesn't refine all the oil it produces, and imports a lot of petrol from other oil-producing countries. As a result, Nigeria misses out on income — crude oil is worth much less than refined oil products like petrol.

4) The oil industry is being held back by Nigeria's poor infrastructure (see below), damage caused to pipelines by theft and protests over the pollution it causes.

Manufacturing industries are Held Back by Poor Infrastructure

1) Although Nigeria has plenty of raw materials and a large labour force that could be used in manufacturing, it makes up a very small part of the economy. This is because:

• Electricity demand exceeds supply so there are frequent power cuts.

• Transport infrastructure is poor. As cities have expanded, the road, rail and shipping network has not kept up causing delays and increasing costs to businesses.

   EXAMPLE: Although Nigeria produces a lot of rubber, tyre company Michelin closed its Nigerian factory in 2007 due to Nigeria's high production costs.

2) The Nigerian government is trying to improve Nigeria's manufacturing sector, for example:

• The government is encouraging foreign companies to build factories in Nigeria by offering them financial incentives.

• Electricity generation has been improved and supplies are starting to increase.

Plenty of industry, but the infrastructure isn't up to the job

It's not enough to just attract foreign companies and keep cities growing — governments also have to make sure the facilities can cope. If the power goes out or every shipment gets stuck in traffic, home-grown companies will suffer and foreign companies will up sticks and leave.

Nigeria — Lagos

Although <u>Abuja</u> is the <u>capital city</u> in Nigeria, <u>Lagos</u> is much, much <u>larger</u>.

Lagos is part of an **Enormous Urban Area**

1) Lagos started as a <u>single settlement</u>, but it has joined up with other settlements to become a huge, <u>sprawling urban area</u>.

2) Estimates of its population vary from <u>8 million</u> to more than <u>22 million</u> depending on how the city is defined.

3) Lagos used to be the capital of Nigeria. Today it is the country's <u>main port</u> and home to <u>several government departments</u>.

Lagos is spread over **Several Islands**

1) Lagos is located at the outlet of the massive <u>Lagos Lagoon</u>, a 50 km long lagoon on the coast of Nigeria.

2) The city started out on <u>Lagos Island</u>, but is now spread around the edge of the lagoon and on some of the other islands.

3) The <u>central business district</u> (CBD) is on Lagos Island. It contains high-rise office buildings, local government headquarters and shops.

4) Lagos is very <u>low lying</u> and is vulnerable to <u>flooding</u>. Many <u>natural wetlands</u> that helped <u>prevent</u> flooding were built on <u>illegally</u> as the city rapidly expanded.

USGS/NASA Landsat

Lagos's Population and Economy are **Growing Rapidly**

1) Lagos attracts a lot of <u>rural-urban migrants</u>. As a result, the city's population has grown <u>faster</u> than the supply of <u>housing</u> can cope with. It's thought that <u>75%</u> of the population live in <u>slums</u> with poor quality <u>housing</u> and <u>no water</u> or <u>sewage</u> services.

2) The influx of migrants from rural areas has also caused an increase in <u>unemployment</u> and the growth of the <u>informal sector</u> (jobs that aren't taxed or regulated by the government).

3) Despite this, Lagos's economy is growing by <u>7%</u> each year.

Lagos is a seaside city with a larger population than Austria

It's Nigeria's largest city, and it's still growing. From a map it looks a bit like Venice, Italy — only the majority of its residents live in <u>slums</u> without <u>reliable water</u> and <u>electricity</u>.

SECTION TEN — A STUDY OF TWO CONTRASTING REGIONS

Japan — Physical Geography

That's enough of Nigeria for now... on to <u>Japan</u>, an <u>MEDC</u> in east Asia.

Japan is a collection of Islands off the East Coast of Asia

1) Japan consists of more than <u>6000 islands</u>, but most of them are <u>uninhabited</u>.

2) The majority of Japan's population live on the <u>four</u> largest islands — <u>Honshu</u>, <u>Hokkaido</u>, <u>Kyushu</u> and <u>Shikoku</u>.

3) In total, it's about <u>50% bigger</u> than the UK.

4) Japan doesn't have many <u>natural resources</u> — it relies on imports.

Most of Japan is Mountainous

1) About <u>80%</u> of Japan's area is <u>mountainous</u> — the <u>tallest</u> mountain is <u>Mt Fuji</u> (3776 m).

2) Towns and cities are mostly on the <u>flatter plains</u> nearer the <u>coast</u>.

3) Because Japan is a long, thin group of islands there are very few long rivers — the <u>longest</u> is the <u>Shinano River</u> on Honshu, which is only <u>367 km long</u>.

4) Most rivers are <u>steep</u> and <u>fast-flowing</u> as they flow out of the mountains.

Japan lies on a Tectonic Plate Boundary

Earthquakes and volcanic eruptions are more likely to occur at plate boundaries (see page 17).

1) Japan is close to where the <u>Pacific</u>, <u>Philippine</u> and <u>Eurasian</u> tectonic plates meet.

2) There have been several major <u>earthquakes</u> in Japan, and the islands are particularly vulnerable to <u>tsunamis</u> (giant waves) caused by earthquakes.

3) Many of Japan's mountains are <u>volcanoes</u>, some of which are still <u>active</u>.

Japan has a Temperate Climate

1) Most of Japan has a <u>temperate climate</u> like the UK — winters are cool, summers are warm and rain occurs throughout the year.

2) There are bits of <u>subtropical</u> climate on the small southern islands though, and Hokkaido is generally <u>colder</u> than the rest of Japan.

3) Vegetation varies — there are <u>evergreen broadleaved</u> trees in the south and <u>deciduous</u> trees in the north. <u>Coniferous</u> trees are found on high ground and in northern parts of Hokkaido.

Japan has lots of islands and mountains

There are a lot of <u>facts</u> to <u>remember</u> here — learn the four main islands and some of Japan's physical characteristics. Have a go at sketching and labelling a map of Japan.

Japan — Population

Japan's population is <u>127 million</u> — it's the 10th most highly populated country in the world. In recent years though, Japan's population has been <u>static</u> or even <u>shrinking</u>.

Japan's **Population** is **Not Growing**

1) In recent years, Japan's population has been <u>static</u> or <u>shrinking</u>.

2) This is because the <u>birth rate</u> (8.1 per 1000 people per year) is <u>lower</u> than the <u>death rate</u> (9.4 per 1000 people per year). The birth rate is one of the <u>lowest</u> in the world.

3) Birth rates are low because couples are having <u>fewer children</u> — couples often choose to save the <u>costs</u> of raising children, or to concentrate on their <u>careers</u>.

4) Death rates are low because the <u>medical services</u> and <u>health care</u> are some of the best in the world.

5) Japan has an <u>ageing population</u> — there are more old people than young people.

6) The literacy rate in Japan is very high — over <u>99%</u>.

These are all indicators of Japan's high level of development.

The **Population Density** is **Highest** in **Urban Areas**

1) The population is <u>not evenly spread out</u> across Japan.

2) Most people live in the big cities with <u>high population densities</u> near the <u>coast</u>. E.g. over a <u>quarter</u> of Japan's population live within the built-up area around <u>Tokyo</u>, the capital of Japan.

3) The number of people living in <u>rural areas</u> in Japan has been <u>decreasing</u> over recent decades.

4) People have been <u>emigrating</u> to the <u>cities</u> and their <u>suburbs</u>. They are attracted to the cities by <u>job opportunities</u> and <u>entertainment</u>.

High population density in Tokyo

Low population density in rural Japan

The **Government** is trying to **Stop** population **Decline**

1) The government in Japan has attempted to increase the country's <u>birth rate</u>.

2) They provide <u>allowances</u> for couples who have children, and have improved <u>working arrangements</u> for parents who have <u>jobs</u>.

3) Permitting more <u>immigration</u> to increase the size of the population is <u>unpopular</u> among Japanese people, so the government has strict rules about who can settle <u>permanently</u>.

Japan's birth rate is low and its population is declining

Japanese people are having <u>fewer children</u> — this means there are a greater proportion of <u>older people</u> in the population, and that the size of the population is <u>shrinking</u>. The government are trying to encourage Japanese people to have more children.

Japan — Farming and Industry

Services and manufacturing are super-important in Japan. Agriculture doesn't get a look-in.

Most people are employed in *Services*

1) Japan's economy is dominated by the service sector. 73% of Japan's income each year comes from services, and 70% of the population are employed in service industries.

2) Some of the most important service industries are retail, transport, finance and business services.

Japan does a **Lot** of **Manufacturing**

1) The manufacturing industries make up about 19% of Japan's income each year.

2) Its main manufacturing industries are a mixture of traditional manufacturing and high-tech industry. They include:

   - Electronics and computers
   - Pharmaceuticals (medical drugs)
   - Petrochemicals (e.g. plastics)
   - Processed food
   - Cars
   - Metal production (e.g. copper and iron)

3) Japan's manufacturing industries (especially traditional industries like shipbuilding) have declined in recent decades due to competition from cheaper foreign firms.

4) They've been replaced by more jobs in services and high-tech firms.

Japan's high-tech industries are backed up by **Research** and **Development**

The quaternary sector is really important for Japan's manufacturing industry — the high-tech products it manufactures are a result of research and development. For example, Japanese electronics giant Sony® spend the equivalent of £2.7 billion on research and development each year.

Farming is **Limited** in Japan

1) Agriculture is not a big part of the economy — it only makes up 1% of Japan's annual income.

2) Nearly half of Japan's food is imported. Most of Japan is steep and rugged, making large-scale farming difficult or impossible.

3) The relatively warm, wet climate and network of rivers means that there is plenty of fresh water for irrigation in much of Japan. This makes growing rice in wet paddy fields possible.

Rice growing in a paddy field

The majority of Japanese people are employed in services

Japan manufactures a lot of stuff, but it also has a very large service sector. What it doesn't do is grow very much food, which is understandable given its shortage of big, flat fields.

Japan — Osaka

Tokyo is the capital of Japan, but <u>Osaka</u> is a large and very important <u>city</u> and <u>port</u>.

*Osaka is located on the **South Coast** of Honshu Island*

Osaka

Tokyo

1) Osaka is the <u>third largest</u> city in Japan.

2) The population of Osaka City is <u>2.5 million</u>, but it is part of the much larger Osaka-Kobe metropolitan area — which has a population of over <u>11.3 million</u> people.

3) Osaka is home to a variety of industries, for example:

- <u>Financial service</u> industries like banks — Osaka is Japan's second largest financial centre.

- <u>Secondary</u> industries — machinery, metal and chemical production is a key industry in the Osaka-Kobe area.

- <u>Trade and export</u> — the Osaka-Kobe port is Japan's largest port for foreign trade.

4) Osaka is famous for its <u>bridges</u>, and for <u>Osaka Castle</u> — a fort that dates back to the 16th century.

*Osaka is built around a **River Delta***

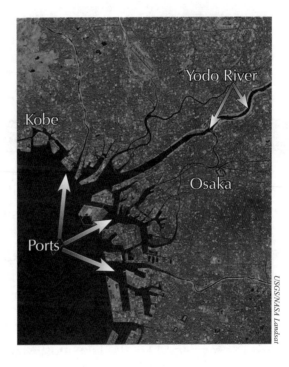

Kobe

Yodo River

Osaka

Ports

USGS/NASA Landsat

1) Osaka is built around the <u>delta</u> of the <u>Yodo River</u>, so there are lots of river channels in the city.

2) Extra space for <u>industry</u> and <u>airports</u> has been <u>reclaimed</u> by building up the delta.

3) The city is <u>low-lying</u> — most of it is less than 15 metres above sea level.

4) This means the city is at risk of <u>flooding</u> from <u>extreme weather</u> caused by typhoons or by tsunamis — although there are <u>flood defences</u> to prevent damage by most storms.

*The city's population is **Declining***

There is a high level of <u>out-migration</u> — people are <u>leaving</u> Osaka's inner city for other urban areas like Tokyo and neighbouring Kobe, and to move out to the suburbs.

Osaka is part of a massive urban area built around a river mouth

2.5 million people live in Osaka, but it goes up to 11.3 million when you add in the urban area that surrounds it. That's a lot of people — it's probably best not to mention the flood risk.

Comparison of Nigeria and Japan

There are lots of <u>differences</u> between Nigeria and Japan.

Nigeria's **Population Growth Rate** is **Positive**, Japan's is **Negative**

Nigeria is a <u>developing</u> country at <u>Stage 2</u> of the <u>Demographic Transition Model</u> (see p.75)

1) The total population of Nigeria is around <u>177 million</u> (the 7th highest in the world).

2) Nigeria's population is still <u>growing</u> very <u>rapidly</u>.

3) Life expectancy is <u>low</u> (53 years) but increasing.

4) Nigeria has a very <u>youthful</u> population (a high proportion of young people).

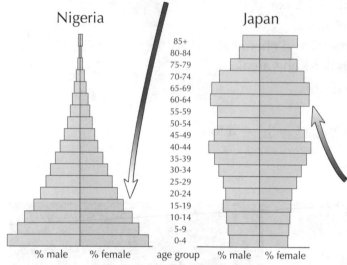

In contrast, Japan is a <u>highly developed</u> country at <u>Stage 4</u> (or possibly Stage 5) of the DTM.

1) Japan's population is <u>127 million</u> (the 10th highest in the world).

2) Japan's population is <u>not growing</u> — it's staying constant or shrinking slowly.

3) Japan's life expectancy is <u>high</u> (84 years).

4) Japan has an <u>ageing</u> population (a high proportion of older people).

The two countries are **Dependent** on **Different Industries**

In Nigeria, a large percentage of the population work in <u>agriculture</u> or <u>services</u> like retail.

1) Most of those in agriculture are <u>subsistence farmers</u> — they grow their own food for their families.

2) Nigeria produces <u>oil</u> and <u>gas</u> and exports most of it for refinement elsewhere. Other industries, including <u>manufacturing</u>, are <u>not</u> <u>growing</u> much due to Nigeria's poor infrastructure.

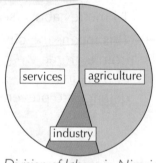

Division of labour in Nigeria

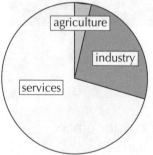

Division of labour in Japan

Japan's economy is dominated by services.

1) Like most MEDCs, Japan has experienced a <u>growth</u> in its <u>service sector</u> over the last 25 years. <u>70%</u> of Japanese people are now employed in services, like retail, finance and transport.

2) Japan's <u>manufacturing</u> sector is declining slowly, but still makes up a fifth of its income — it produces a lot of high-tech electronics, computers, cars and medical drugs.

3) <u>Agriculture</u> employs a very <u>small</u> fraction of the population, and makes up just over <u>1%</u> of Japan's income.

Nigeria (like many LEDCs) <u>imports</u> mainly <u>manufactured</u> or <u>processed</u> products like <u>cars</u> and <u>industrial equipment</u>, and exports <u>crude oil</u>. Japan (like many MEDCs) <u>imports fuels</u> and <u>raw materials</u> and exports <u>manufactured goods</u>, especially high-tech products.

Comparison of Nigeria and Japan

The **Physical Geography** of both countries is different

1) Nigeria is a country that has <u>several different</u> natural environments — mangroves, tropical rainforests and savanna grasslands.

2) <u>Two</u> very <u>long rivers</u> flow through Nigeria — the Niger and the Benue.

3) Nigeria isn't very mountainous — large areas of the country are <u>relatively flat</u>.

4) Japan's islands have very different <u>vegetation</u> to Nigeria, with a variety of evergreen broadleaved trees, deciduous trees and coniferous trees.

5) Japan's rivers are all <u>short</u> — the islands mean no river source is far from the sea.

6) Japan is very <u>mountainous</u> — around 80% of the country is made up of highlands.

Their **Climates** are **Different**

The <u>climates</u> of Nigeria and Japan differ because of their <u>locations</u> in the world. They're both in the northern hemisphere, but Nigeria is <u>near</u> the <u>equator</u> and Japan is much <u>further north</u>.

- <u>Nigeria</u> has a <u>more varied</u> climate than Japan. It varies from hot and humid with heavy rainfall along the coast, to hot and more arid further inland.

- In comparison, <u>Japan</u> mostly has <u>one type</u> of climate — a <u>temperate climate</u> similar to that of the UK. The average temperature in Japan is quite cool in comparison to Nigeria, although the south of Japan does enjoy <u>hot summers</u>.

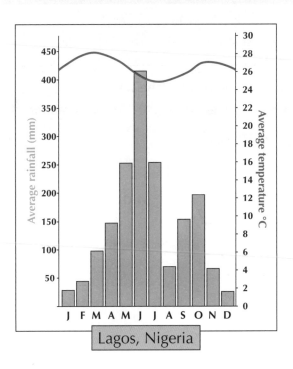

Lagos, Nigeria

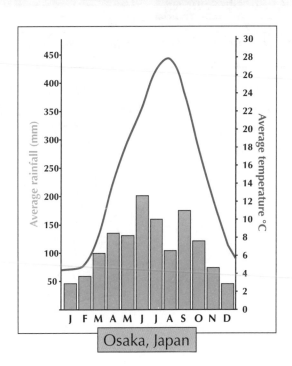

Osaka, Japan

Nigeria and Japan have very different climates...

... because they are in <u>different places</u>. Japan is a lot further from the equator, so it gets a lot colder in the winter. But parts of Nigeria are a lot more rainy, which is handy for its rainforests.

Questions

Well I bet you know a lot more about Nigeria and Japan now than you did before you'd ever laid eyes on section ten. There's only one way to work out how much more you know now — you guessed it, it's time for some questions.

Warm-up Questions

1) In which continent is Nigeria?

2) What sort of climate does most of Nigeria have?

3) Is Nigeria's population increasing or decreasing?

4) What makes up most of Nigeria's exports?

5) Is Lagos's economy growing, shrinking or staying constant?

6) Describe where Japan is in the world.

7) What is happening to the size of Japan's population?

8) Which sector makes up most of Japan's annual income?

9) Name the river that flows through Osaka.

10) Which country is further north, Nigeria or Japan?

Practice Questions

Don't be afraid to take your time over these practice questions — they're a bit tricky.

1) Look at the map of Nigeria below. Match the words to the correct labels.

Savanna grassland   **Benue River**   **Mangroves**   **Niger River**   **Tropical rainforest**

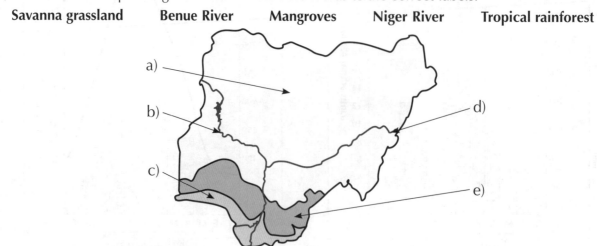

2) Copy out the passage below, using the correct option from each pair.

Nigeria's birth rate is (**high / low**) and the death rate is also (**high / low**), but not as (**high / low**) as the birth rate. This means that the population is (**shrinking / growing**).

Questions

3) Which two of the statements below describe why manufacturing is being held back in Nigeria?

   A   The transport infrastructure isn't good enough.

   B   There aren't enough raw materials in Nigeria.

   C   There isn't enough power being generated.

   D   There aren't enough people able to work in Nigeria.

   E   It's difficult to get permission from the government to open a factory.

4) Copy and complete the passage below using the words supplied.

   mountainous   temperate   6000   tectonic plate   the UK   tropical   Nigeria

   There are over _____ islands in Japan. It's a very _____ country, and it lies on
   a _____ boundary. Japan has a _____ climate like _____.

5) Which of the following statements are true? Write corrections for any that are false.

   A Osaka is the largest city in Japan.

   B Osaka is part of a large urban area home to over 11 million people.

   C Osaka is very low-lying and vulnerable to flooding.

   D The population of Osaka city is growing rapidly.

6) Give two ways in which the cities of Osaka and Lagos are similar.

7) Look at the climate graphs below.

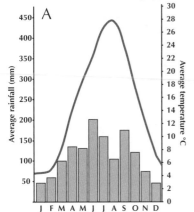
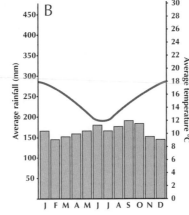
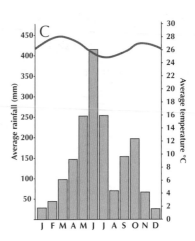

   a) Which graph shows the climate of Lagos, Nigeria?

   b) Which graph shows the climate of Osaka, Japan?

Section Ten — Summary Questions

Nearly done — just one more page of questions on Nigeria and Japan to go, then you can disappear into the wonderful world of geographical skills in section eleven. Here are a few summary questions to make sure you've got all the details from your contrasting regions sorted. If there are some you can't answer, have another read of this section — all the answers are there.

1) What are mangroves?

2) Where in Nigeria is rainforest vegetation found?

3) Which type of environment makes up most of Nigeria?

4) Name the two largest rivers in Nigeria.

5) What is the population of Nigeria?

6) Does Nigeria have a young, middle-aged or ageing population?

7) Give two reasons why the south of Nigeria is densely populated.

8) Which sector of the economy do nearly half of all Nigerians work in?

9) Give one factor that is holding back Nigeria's oil industry.

10) Name the island that Lagos's Central Business District is on.

11) What is the tallest mountain in Japan?

12) Why is Japan vulnerable to earthquakes and volcanic eruptions?

13) Why are migrants attracted to cities like Tokyo from the rural areas that surround them?

14) What makes up 73% of Japan's income?

15) Name three of Japan's main manufacturing industries.

16) How much of Japan's food is imported?

17) Which island is Osaka on?

18) Around which river's delta is Osaka built?

19) Describe the differences between Nigeria and Japan's population pyramids.

20) Give one thing that Nigeria imports a lot of.

21) Give one thing that Japan imports a lot of.

22) Name one thing that Japan exports.

23) Which country is more mountainous, Nigeria or Japan?

24) Which city has more variation between summer and winter temperatures, Lagos, Nigeria or Osaka, Japan?

What is Geographical Enquiry?

Geographers love geographical enquiries so you need to know what they are.

A geographical enquiry is an **Investigation** of a **Topic** or **Matter**

Geographical enquiry involves people asking geographical questions about an issue or a problem. There are a number of important key questions that should be used in a geographical enquiry:

> WHAT?   WHERE?   HOW?   WHY?   WHO?

Geographers apply these enquiry questions to a local issue or a global issue.

A geographical enquiry begins with **Questioning**

Once the information produced from the questioning has been collected, the information is presented and analysed. There's loads of different ways to conduct a geographical enquiry. Here's an example of how you would normally go about doing one —

Questioning → Information Collection → Information Presentation → Information Analysis

To help you understand a bit more here's two examples of the questions that could be asked:

A **Local Issue** — e.g. traffic congestion

There is traffic congestion in your local town centre during the day.
The key questions that might be asked in a geographical enquiry are:

- What is happening to the traffic?
- Where are the main traffic problems?
- Why is the traffic a problem?
- Who is affected by the traffic?
- How is the traffic problem being dealt with?

A **Global Issue** — e.g. deforestation in the Amazon Rainforest

Deforestation is taking place in the Amazon rainforest. The key questions that might be asked in a geographical enquiry are:

- Where is the tropical rainforest located?
- What is happening to the tropical rainforest?
- How is the rainforest changing?
- Why is the rainforest changing?
- Who is responsible for these changes?
- What possible solutions are there to these problems?

Geographical enquiry is just a fancy way to say studying an issue

To get your data you ask a load of questions (what? where? how? why? and who?) and record the answers. Then you collect it all up, present and interpret it... easy.

Sources of Information

There are lots of different sources of information that can be used in a geographical enquiry. Information is also called 'data' and there are two main types.

1) Primary Data is information that you Collect Yourself

This might be collected by asking people questions or counting.

Here are some examples of primary data sources:

1) A questionnaire asks people a set of questions about their opinion on a particular topic, e.g. shopping. You could give a questionnaire to your schoolmates, people on the street or post them out to people.

2) A traffic count is when you count the number of vehicles per hour or per minute on a particular road. Often with a traffic count, you divide the types of vehicles into categories so you might count the number of motorbikes, cars, lorries, buses and bicycles.

3) A pedestrian count is when you count the number of people who pass you per hour or per minute. To do a pedestrian count you need to stand still in one place and count the people who walk past you. The place might be outside a cinema or a leisure centre.

4) A land use survey is a survey of how the land is used in an area. You need to get a map of an area and use a colour code to identify how each piece of land is used, e.g. for housing or shopping or a park area. You can also do a land use survey of places like shopping centres, to see the different types of shops in the centre.

5) An environmental quality survey is an assessment of how good or bad the quality of the environment is in an area. You might assess how clean an area is by looking at the amount of litter on the floor. You can give the cleanliness of an area a mark out of 5, where 5 is very clean and 1 is very dirty.

2) Secondary Data is information from Another Source

This might be information that you have collected from the TV, internet, books or newspapers.

Here are some examples of secondary data sources:

1) Web sites on the internet — e.g. you could look at government web sites that contain census data. The census is a survey carried out every 10 years that all households must fill in. The data from it gives us lots of information about the UK population.

2) Books from the library — you could use map books, journals and birth or death registers.

3) Stories or statistics in newspapers — local newspapers would be useful sources of information if you were doing a local project.

4) Maps — you could use Ordnance Survey® maps, local street maps, globes or atlases to help you locate features in your enquiry.

You collect primary data yourself, secondary comes from other sources

You can get information from loads of different sources, you don't always have to collect it yourself. Don't forget that 'data' and 'information' are the same thing here.

Geographical Enquiry

We can answer a range of enquiry questions by analysing and evaluating other sources of data — for example, graphs, maps, statistics and publicity leaflets.

Graphs can be a good Source of Data

A variety of different graphs can be valuable sources of data in geographical enquiries — pie charts, line graphs, scatter graphs, bar graphs, pictographs and divided bar graphs (see further on in this section for more on types of graphs). Pie charts can be a useful data source because they show percentage data and they are easier to read than other graphs.

Maps show Distributions

Maps are excellent sources of data for analysis and evaluation in geographical enquiry because they show distributions. For example, the results from a traffic count could be shown on a map and this would highlight the roads in an area with traffic problems. Maps are also used to present land use survey data. Annotated maps are also really useful — they have labels and notes included on them.

Statistical Data shows Trends

Statistical data ranges from tally charts to complex tests. Statistical data is useful to spot trends over time, for example, increases or decreases in the amount of people using a particular facility like out-of-town shopping centres or what the most and least popular ways of getting to school are.

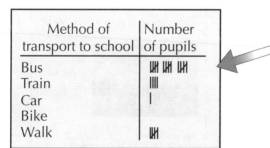

Method of transport to school	Number of pupils
Bus	ЖЖ ЖЖ ЖЖ
Train	IIII
Car	I
Bike	
Walk	ЖЖ

This tally chart shows that most pupils go to school on the bus and no pupils cycle to school.

Publicity Leaflets show people's Point of View

Publicity leaflets can be analysed and evaluated in a geographical enquiry. Publicity leaflets usually give a range of different views and opinions about an issue. You might get publicity leaflets from the tourist information centre, the council or from companies. You need to be careful though — sometimes the information is biased towards one viewpoint.

For example, the owners of a supermarket that plan to open in the area may produce a leaflet for local people, explaining only the benefits of the new supermarket. However, the council may produce a leaflet on the same issue to show a balanced perspective on the new development.

Don't forget that some sources of data might be biased

Graphs, maps and statistics all show distributions and trends so aren't generally biased — but watch out for bias in leaflets, having a look at who produced it should help.

Geographical Enquiry

You can <u>communicate</u> your data and findings to other people in lots of <u>different ways</u>.

You **Could Write** about the issue

A geographical enquiry can be communicated to people in <u>writing</u>, e.g. writing a report on the issue. When you're writing about an issue try to do the following things:

1) Use the most <u>up-to-date</u> information you have.
2) Write about <u>both sides</u> of the story — try to include everyone's viewpoint.
3) Give <u>examples</u> to illustrate your point.
4) <u>Explain</u> any <u>technical terms</u> you use.
5) Include any <u>background information</u> you think might be needed.
6) Suggest <u>sources</u> for <u>further information</u>.

You **Could** also produce a **Leaflet**

When you've done a geographical enquiry a <u>leaflet</u> could be produced that <u>tells people about what you've found out</u>.

' There's loads of things you could include:

1) <u>Writing</u>
2) <u>Photographs</u>
3) <u>Annotated maps</u>
4) <u>Graphs</u>
5) <u>Statistics</u>

For example, a leaflet produced on the Congestion Charge in London could contain lots of information about what it is, where it is and its advantages and disadvantages. A leaflet might include a written description of the Congestion Charge with some photographs, statistics and a location map.

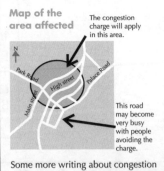

Congestion Charge

This is a photograph of the traffic jams in London.

This is a leaflet. This is a leaflet. This is a leaflet. This is a leaflet. This is a leaflet. This is a leaflet. This is a leaflet. This is a leaflet. This is a leaflet. This is a leaflet. This is a leaflet. This is a leaflet. This is a leaflet. This is a leaflet. This is a leaflet. This is a leaflet. This is a leaflet. This is a leaflet. This is a leaflet. This is a leaflet.

Map of the area affected

The congestion charge will apply in this area.

Park Road · High street · Palace Road · Main street

This road may become very busy with people avoiding the charge.

Some more writing about congestion charges. Some more writing about congestion charges. Some more writing about congestion charges. Some more writing about congestion charges. Some more writing about

Try and make your leaflet <u>tidy</u> and <u>presentable</u> — use a ruler to draw lines and write neatly. If you have <u>desktop publishing</u> software at home or at school, try doing it on that.

How you communicate your data depends on the task and audience

The way you communicate data needs to be appropriate — for example if you were telling local people where flooding is likely to occur, an annotated map would be the most useful way.

Questions

Those four pages weren't too bad. Geographical enquiry might seem complicated at first but once you've gone over the pages a few times it'll become clearer. Just think about what you want to work out, what data you need to collect and how you're going to present, analyse and communicate it to other people.

Warm-up Questions

1) What does a geographical enquiry involve?

2) What is data?

3) Give one example of a primary data source and one example of a secondary data source.

4) Give two ways that you could communicate your findings to other people.

Practice Questions

Just three short practice questions for you now... nothing too difficult.

1) Copy and complete these sentences:

Primary data is information collected by **(yourself / others)**.

Secondary data is information collected by **(yourself / others)**.

A traffic count is an example of **(primary / secondary)** data.

2) Are the statements below about geographical enquiry true or false?

a) A pie chart is the most suitable graph to present all types of data.

b) There are lots of different graphs that can be used to present data.

c) The data collected can answer lots of enquiry questions.

d) There is no need to analyse the data once it has been presented.

3) Copy and complete these sentences with the words below:

vehicles   traffic   pedestrian   people   population   questions

A questionnaire asks people a set of _____ about a particular topic.

A traffic count is when you count the number of _____ per hour or per minute on a particular road.

A _____ count is when you count the number of people who pass you per hour or per minute.

Census data can tell you information about the _____.

Ordnance Survey Maps

The next three pages tell you all about OS® maps. You need to learn it so you know how to find places, describe places and navigate — then you won't get lost when you go on field-trips.

Know your Compass Points

You've got to know the compass — for giving <u>directions</u>, saying which way a <u>river's flowing</u>, or knowing what they mean if your teacher says 'look at the river in the <u>north-west</u> of the map'. Read it <u>out loud</u> to yourself, going <u>clockwise</u>.

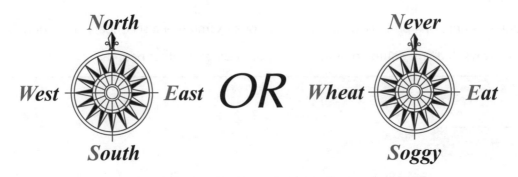

The Scale of a map helps you work out Distances

Maps are <u>scaled</u> — they're <u>smaller</u> than in <u>real life</u>, e.g. if a scale is 1:50 000, distances on the map are 50 000 times smaller than in real life.

To work out the <u>distance</u> between two features, use a <u>ruler</u> to measure in <u>cm</u> and then <u>compare</u> it to the scale to work out the distance in <u>km</u>.

Example

The churches are 3.4 cm apart on the map...

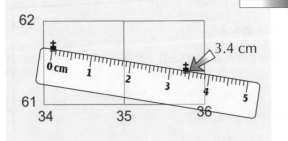

If you want to measure the length of a road or a river, lie a piece of string along it, then measure the piece of string and do the same as you would with a ruler.

1) Put your ruler next to the scale, so the 0 on the scale lines up with the 3.4 on the ruler.

2) Then go along to 0 on the ruler and read off the value on the scale (1.7 km in this example).

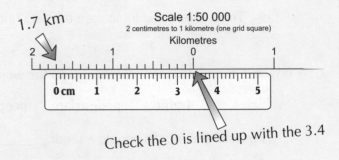

Check the 0 is lined up with the 3.4

...which means the churches are 1.7 km apart in real life.

Remember to compare your ruler measurement to the scale

You need to repeat the compass points to yourself until you know them good and well. And make sure you always use a ruler when working out distances — guessing just won't do.

Ordnance Survey Maps

Grid references are a <u>set of numbers</u> that you use to <u>locate a place</u> on a map.

Grid References *tell you where something is*

There are two types of grid reference — a <u>four</u>-figure reference and a <u>six</u>-figure reference.
Here's how you work them out, using the Post Office® in the map below as an example:

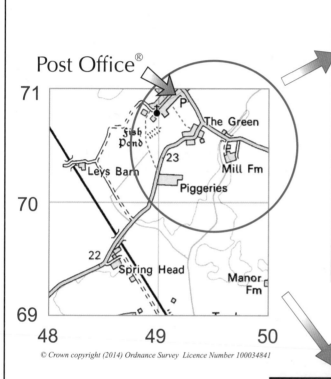

© *Crown copyright (2014) Ordnance Survey Licence Number 100034841*

FOUR-Figure Grid References

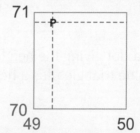

1) Find the square with the Post Office® in.

2) Find the <u>Eastings</u> (across) value for the <u>left</u> side of the square — <u>49</u>.

3) Find the <u>Northings</u> (up) value for the <u>bottom</u> of the square — <u>70</u>.

4) Write the numbers together, Eastings first. The grid reference is <u>4970</u>.

SIX-Figure Grid References

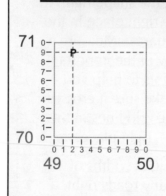

1) Start by working out the <u>basic</u> Eastings and Northings as above.

2) Then imagine the square's divided into <u>tenths</u>. Divide it by <u>eye</u> — or even better use your <u>ruler</u>.

3) The Eastings value is now <u>492</u> (49 and 2 "tenths") and the Northings is <u>709</u> (70 and 9 "tenths").

4) The six-figure reference is <u>492709</u>.

<u>Always</u> write the numbers down in the <u>right order</u>.
The Golden Rule: "<u>FIRST</u> choose a number from the bottom edge of the map."

Remember — find the 'across' value first, then the 'up' value

You work out four-figure and six-figure references basically the same way, the only difference is that the six-figure one is more accurate than the four-figure reference.

Ordnance Survey Maps

The *Relief* of an area is shown by *Contours* and *Spot Heights*

1) <u>Contours</u> are those orange lines on Ordnance Survey® maps.
   They're imaginary lines joining points of <u>equal height</u> above sea-level.

2) If a map has <u>lots</u> of contour lines on it, it's a <u>hilly</u> or <u>mountainous area</u>.
   If there are only a few contour lines, it'll be <u>flat</u>, and usually <u>low-lying</u>.

3) The <u>steeper</u> the slope is, the <u>closer</u> the contours get. The <u>flatter</u> it is,
   the more <u>spaced out</u> they are. Look at these examples:

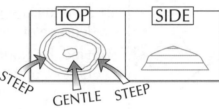

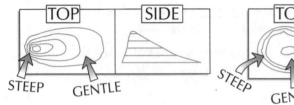

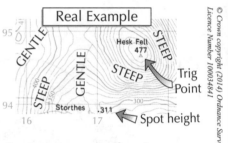

4) A <u>spot height</u> is a dot giving the <u>height</u> of a particular place. A <u>trigonometrical point</u>
   (trig point) is a blue triangle plus a height value, showing the <u>highest point</u> in an area
   (in metres).

© Crown copyright (2014) Ordnance Survey Licence Number 100034841

Sketching Maps — *do it Carefully*

1) Your teacher might ask you to sketch a map.

2) Make sure you <u>check what bit</u> they want you to draw out.
   It might be only <u>part</u> of a lake or a wood, or only <u>one</u> of the roads.

3) Draw your sketch <u>in pencil</u> so you can rub it out if it's wrong.

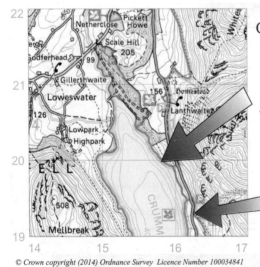

© Crown copyright (2014) Ordnance Survey Licence Number 100034841

Get the <u>shape</u> right, in the <u>right place</u> in the squares. <u>Measure</u> a few of the <u>important points</u> to help you — make sure it crosses the <u>grid lines</u> in the right place.

Get <u>widths</u> of any <u>roads</u> right.

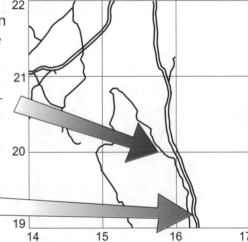

4) See if you can lay the grid over the map — then you can <u>trace</u> bits of it.

The closer the contour lines, the steeper the hill

Don't let numbers on maps fox you — remember the difference between spot heights and trig points and you should be safe. And don't be slapdash when sketching maps.

Human Geography — Plans and Photos

Plans, like maps, show things from above. And like maps, there are a few tricks you need to learn.

Look at the **Shapes** when you compare **Plans** and **Photos**

1) The simplest question your teacher could ask you is "*Name the place labelled A on the photo*". Names are on the plan, so you've got to work out how the photo matches the plan.

2) The plan and map might not be the same way up, so watch out. Look for the main features on the photo and find them on the plan — things with an interesting shape like a lake, or big roads and railways.

<u>EXAMPLE ONE</u>

Question — *Name the place labelled A on the photo.*

Answer — *By the shape of the land, it's either got to be Hope Point or Dead Dog Point. There isn't a road or building at point A, so it can't be Dead Dog Point — it must be Hope Point.*

Photograph of St. James Harbour, 1986

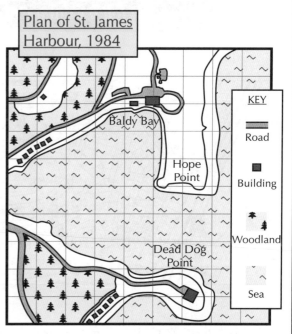

Plan of St. James Harbour, 1984

3) The other type of question you might be asked is what's changed between the photo and the plan, and why. Look at the shapes to find what's changed, then look at what it's being used for now (check the dates).

<u>EXAMPLE TWO</u>

Question — *Where has land been reclaimed from the sea?*

Answer — *By the shape of the land, it's got to be Baldy Bay — the sea's much further from that building now. It's now being used as a car park.*

Don't be too quick to answer questions on this — think carefully

This page looks a bit fiddly, but it's all simple advice. It's easy to match a photo to the wrong part of the plan by mistake — so don't worry if you don't get it first time round.

Human Geography — Plans and Photos

Plans of Towns and Aerial Photos — look at the Buildings

1) When you're studying a plan, start by looking at the types of buildings and what's around them.

2) Small buildings are probably houses or shops. Bigger buildings are probably factories or schools.

3) Work out what kind of area it is — lots of car parks and shops usually mean it's a CBD, houses with gardens mean a residential area, a group of houses surrounded by fields means a village. Always read the labels, they can give you a lot of easy clues.

> **EXAMPLE:** *This area has houses with front and back gardens, a park, a school and a college. So it's a residential area — you can tell it's not a CBD and not dense inner-city housing.*

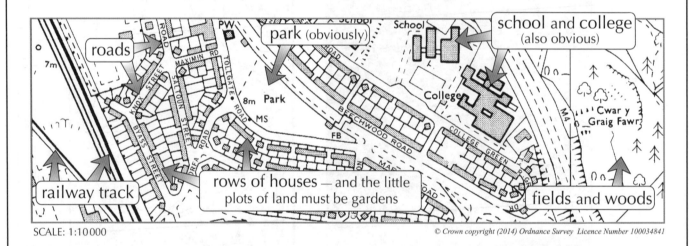

SCALE: 1:10 000

© Crown copyright (2014) Ordnance Survey Licence Number 100034841

AERIAL PHOTOS: if you get an aerial photo instead of a plan, treat it in exactly the same way — look for types of buildings and what kind of area it is. You can see the cars and trees which helps, but there won't be any labels.

> **EXAMPLE:** *This area has tall buildings that are densely packed together, and what looks like a cathedral. So it's probably a city centre (in fact it's London city centre).*

This is mostly common sense

Look at the plan you're given and try to assess how areas within the plan differ. You need to check for clues — buildings, roads, rail tracks, open spaces. Keep your eyes peeled.

Questions

There's quite a bit to take in from the last five pages. Take your time and make sure you understand it all. Same routine as usual here, try the warm-up questions then move onto the practice ones when you're ready.

Warm-up Questions

1) Sketch a circle and mark the four compass points on it.

2) Describe how you would find a four-figure grid reference on a map.

3) Does a steep slope have contour lines that are far apart or close together?

4) On part of a town plan or aerial photograph, how could you tell if an area is:

   a) a CBD;   b) a residential area;   c) a village?

Practice Questions

Here are two quick practice questions just to keep you on your toes.

1) Look at this map of Leyburn. Then answer the questions underneath it.

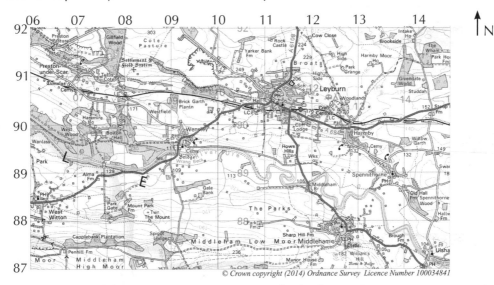

© Crown copyright (2014) Ordnance Survey Licence Number 100034841

   a) Which one of these two squares contains the highest point — 1390 or 1191?

   b) Which one of these two squares has the steepest slope — 1288 or 0788?

   c) If you walked along the road from 092878 to 093883, would you be going uphill or downhill?

   d) If you walked along the road from 090893 to 092880, would you be going uphill or downhill?

2) Find these three buildings on the map then answer the questions below:
   Gale Bank — 096885, Harmby Moor House — 133912, and Brough Farm — 141876.

   a) Which building is on a north-facing slope?

   b) Which building is most likely to flood?

Describing Maps and Charts

You might be asked by your teacher or in a test to describe <u>distributions</u> and <u>photos</u>. This can seem a bit difficult, but it's pretty easy once you've got the hang of it.

Distributions on Maps — keep it Simple

Here's an example question:

Q1   *Use the map to describe the distribution of areas*
       with a population density less than 10 persons per km^2.

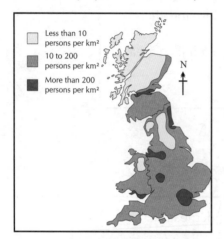

Questions like this can be tough — you can <u>see</u> where those light grey patches are, but putting it into <u>words</u> seems silly. <u>Don't panic</u> — just write down <u>a description of where things are</u>.

A WORKED EXAMPLE:

"The areas with a population density less than 10 persons per km^2 are distributed in the <u>north of Scotland</u>, the <u>north</u> and <u>south-west</u> of <u>England</u>, and <u>northern Wales</u>."

ANOTHER WORKED EXAMPLE:

Q2   *Use the maps to describe the distribution of National Parks in Spondovia.*

They've given you <u>two maps</u>, which means they want you to look at them <u>both</u>. Look at the <u>first map</u> and say <u>where the blobs are</u>, then look at the <u>second map</u> and say <u>if there's any link</u> or not:

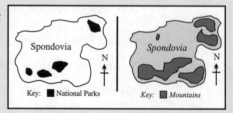

"The National Parks are distributed in the <u>south-west</u> and <u>north-east</u> of Spondovia. They are all located in <u>mountainous</u> areas."

The best plan is to actually practise answering questions like these

It's really not that bad. You just need to read the question you're given carefully before you jump in with an answer. Make sure your answer is short and to the point.

Describing Maps and Charts

Describing Photographs — check what you need to describe

1) <u>Double-check</u> what the question's asking. <u>Don't</u> tell them <u>everything</u> about a subject if they're only asking about what you can see in the photo — you <u>won't</u> get extra marks.

Look at these two examples for this photo:

> *"The photo shows a 'honey-pot'. List the factors that attract tourists to honey-pot locations."*
>
> This is asking you to tell them <u>everything</u> you know about honey-pots.
>
> *"The photo shows a 'honey-pot'. List three factors that would attract tourists to this location."*
>
> This is asking you to list <u>only</u>
> the things you can <u>see</u> in <u>this photo</u>.

2) If you're asked what you can <u>see</u> in the photo, then <u>don't over-complicate</u> things — stick to what you can <u>see</u> in the photo. For example, if they asked how <u>people</u> are affecting <u>erosion</u> of cliffs in this photo, then it's by <u>walking</u> on them (the footpath), <u>not</u> the cars causing acid rain or something.

3) When you get a photo, look for <u>physical geography stuff</u> (what the land's like), e.g. <u>coastal features</u> and <u>river features</u>, and the <u>human geography stuff</u> (what the land is used for), e.g. the types of <u>buildings</u>, if there are any <u>car parks</u>, if there are <u>roads</u> or <u>paths</u>, etc.

4) Use your head — for example if it <u>looks nice</u> and there's a <u>car park</u>, you can guess there'll be <u>tourism</u>.

Double-check what you're being asked to do...

...that way you won't get the wrong end of the stick and write a whole essay when all you had to do was write a few sentences.

Types of Graphs and Charts

There are two things you need to be able to do with graphs:

1) know how to <u>read</u> all of the types of graphs.
2) know how to <u>fill in</u> all of the types of graphs.

*Bar Charts — draw the bars **Straight** and **Neat***

Bar charts are pretty simple really:

1) How to Read Bar Charts

1) Read along the <u>bottom</u> to find the <u>bar</u> you want.
2) Read from the <u>top</u> of the bar across to the <u>scale</u>, and read off the number.

EXAMPLE:

Q: How many tonnes of oil does Breitland produce per year?

A: Go up the Breitland bar, read across, and it's about 620 on the scale — but the scale's in thousands of tonnes, so the answer is <u>620 000 tonnes</u>.

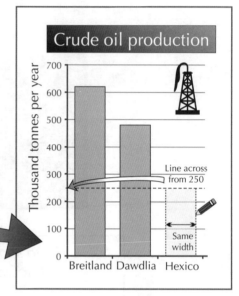

Crude oil production

2) How to Fill In Bar Charts

1) First find the number you want on the <u>vertical scale</u>. With a <u>ruler</u>, trace a line across.
2) Draw in a bar of the <u>right size</u> — use a <u>ruler</u> or it'll look messy.

EXAMPLE:

Q: Complete the graph to show that Hexico produces 250 thousand tonnes per year.

A: Find 250 on the scale, trace a line across, then draw the bar in, the <u>same width</u> as the others.

Make sure you've got the essentials — ruler and sharp pencils

You've probably had to use bar charts in other subjects, so this should be pretty familiar. Spend some time making your graphs clear and neat — that way everyone'll be able to read them.

Types of Graphs and Charts

Line Graphs — *the points are joined by* **Lines**

1) How to Read Line Graphs

1) Read along the <u>bottom</u> to find the number you want.

2) Read up to the line you want, then read across to the <u>vertical scale</u>.

EXAMPLE:

Q: How much coal did the north of England produce in 1919?

A: Find 1919, go up to the purple line, read across, and it's 50 on the scale. The scale's in millions of tonnes, so the answer is <u>50 million tonnes</u>.

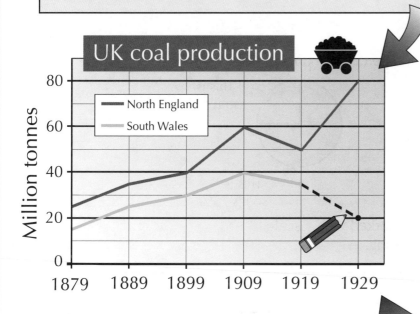

UK coal production

2) How to Fill In Line Graphs

1) Find the value you want on the <u>bottom scale</u>.

2) Go up to get the right value on the <u>vertical scale</u>. <u>Double-check</u> you're still at the right value from the <u>bottom</u>, then make a <u>mark</u>.

3) Using a <u>ruler</u>, join the mark to the line.

EXAMPLE:

Q: Complete the graph to show that South Wales produced 20 million tonnes in 1929.

A: Find 1929 on the bottom, then go up to 20 million tonnes and make a mark, then join it to the green line <u>with a ruler</u>.

Look at some real line graphs and test yourself

Something to watch out for with these charts and graphs is reading the <u>scale</u> — check how much each division is <u>worth</u> — sometimes they're worth one, sometimes they're worth more.

Types of Graphs and Charts

Pie charts are a way of showing <u>percentages</u>.

Pie Charts show Percentages

1) How to Read Pie Charts

Read numbers off a <u>pie chart with a scale</u> like this:

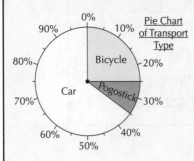

1) To work out the % for a wedge, write down where it <u>starts</u> and <u>ends</u>, then <u>subtract</u>.

2) For example, the 'Car' wedge goes from 35% to 100%: 100 − 35 = <u>65%</u>

You could be asked to <u>estimate</u> the percentage on a pie chart <u>without a scale</u>:

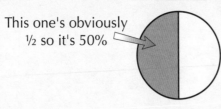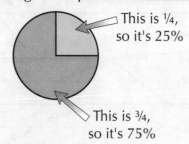

This one's obviously ½ so it's 50%

This is ¼, so it's 25%

This is ¾, so it's 75%

If there's another pie chart that <u>is</u> marked with a scale, use it to <u>help you</u> with your estimating.

2) How to Fill In Pie Charts

1) With a <u>ruler</u>, draw lines from the <u>centre</u> to <u>0%</u>, and to the number on the <u>outside</u> that you want. Here's how you'd do <u>45%</u>:

2) To do <u>another</u> wedge, you'd have to <u>start</u> from <u>45%</u>. So, if the wedge needed to be, say <u>20%</u>, it'd end on 45 + 20 = <u>65%</u>.

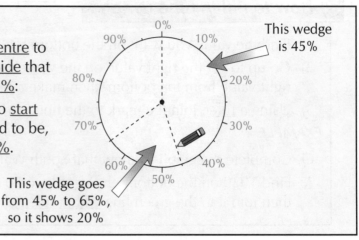

This wedge is 45%

This wedge goes from 45% to 65%, so it shows 20%

Remember — you've got to label your pie chart once you've drawn it

Pie charts are just about showing percentages in a diagram. Again, you need to test yourself to make sure you know it. This means both <u>reading</u> pie charts and <u>drawing</u> them yourself.

Types of Graphs and Charts

Triangular Graphs show Percentages too — on 3 Axes

Let's be honest, triangular graphs look like a <u>nightmare</u> at first. But they're actually fairly <u>easy</u> to use.

1) How to Read Triangular Graphs

1) Find the point you want on the graph. <u>Turn the paper</u> so that one set of numbers is the <u>right way up</u>. Follow the lines <u>straight across</u> to that set of numbers, and write it down.

2) Keep turning the paper round for <u>each set</u> of numbers.

3) <u>Double-check</u> that the numbers you've written down add up to 100%.

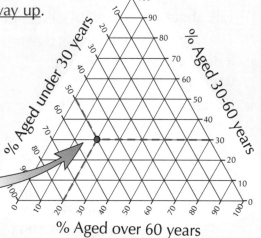

EXAMPLE:

This point shows a population where <u>50%</u> are aged under 30, <u>30%</u> aged 30-60, and <u>20%</u> aged over 60. Double-check they add to 100%: 50 + 30 + 20 = 100%. <u>Good</u>.

% Aged over 60 years

2) How to Fill In Triangular Graphs

1) Start with <u>one set</u> of numbers — <u>turn the paper round</u> till they're the right way up. Find the number you want, then draw a <u>faint pencil line</u> straight across.

2) Do the same for the other sets of numbers, <u>turning the paper round</u> each time.

3) Where your three lines <u>meet</u>, draw a <u>dot</u>.

4) <u>Double-check</u> your dot's in the right place — follow the steps for <u>reading</u> triangular graphs.

Always double-check the numbers you've written add up to 100

You don't get triangular graphs in everyday life, but you might use them in lessons or for a piece of coursework — so learn them well. The secret is to <u>turn the paper round</u> each time.

Types of Graphs and Charts

Describing what Graphs Show — look for the Important Bits

The phrase "*Describe what is shown by the graph*" might seem petrifying — but what you actually need to <u>do</u> is <u>easy</u>. Read on.

The Four things to look for

1) Talk about bits where it's <u>going up</u>.
2) Talk about where it's <u>going down</u>.
3) If there's a <u>peak</u> (highest bit), write that down.
4) If there's a <u>trough</u> (lowest bit), write that down.

EXAMPLE:

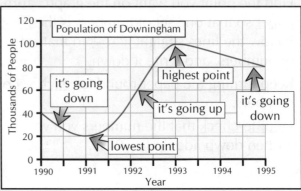

"The population fell between 1990 and 1991, then increased until 1993 when it began to fall again. The population was highest in 1993 at 100 000, and was lowest in 1991 at 20 000."

Scatter Graphs — draw a Best Fit Line and talk about the correlation

With a bit of luck, any scatter graphs will already have a best fit line on them. If not, <u>sketch your own</u> in roughly the right place, then write down what type of 'correlation' there is:

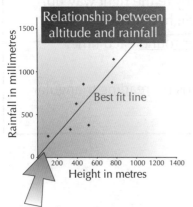

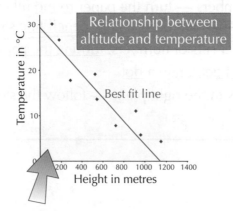

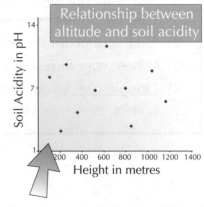

As height increases, rainfall also increases. The line slopes <u>up</u> from <u>left to right</u> — there is a "<u>positive correlation</u>".

As height increases, temperature decreases. The line is sloping <u>down</u> to the <u>right</u> — there's a "<u>negative correlation</u>".

There is no link between height and soil acidity. When there's <u>no correlation</u>, you can't draw a line of best fit.

This is vital stuff — don't skim over it

Describing graphs isn't a problem if you have a checklist of things to look for — up, down, peak, trough. And make sure you don't get the terms for describing scatter graphs mixed up.

Types of Graphs and Charts

Two completely different types of <u>map</u> here, both with ridiculously complicated names — <u>topological</u> maps and <u>choropleth</u> maps. You don't need to remember the names, just <u>what they're for</u> and <u>how they work</u>.

Topological Maps show how to get from *Place* to *Place*

1) Topological maps show <u>transport</u> connections. They're often used to explain <u>rail</u> and <u>underground networks</u>.

2) It's highly unlikely you'll have to <u>draw</u> a topological map.

3) If you have to <u>read</u> a topological map just remember the <u>dots</u> are <u>places</u>. The <u>lines</u> show <u>routes</u> between the places.

4) If two lines cross <u>at a dot</u> then it's a place where you can <u>switch</u> from one route to another.

5) Always check out the <u>key</u>.

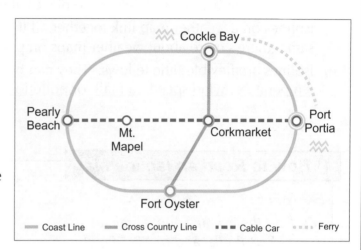

Choropleth Maps use *Hatched Lines*, *Dots* or *Colours*

Another strange name for you: '<u>choropleth</u>' — it's not as complicated as it sounds, you just need to be able to use a key. Get the '<u>describing graphs</u>' bit sorted — it's really important.

1) Choropleth maps use <u>crosshatched lines</u>, <u>dots</u> or <u>colours</u> to represent different areas.

2) They're very straightforward to use, but all those lines can start to look a bit complicated.

3) If you're asked to talk about all the bits of the map with a <u>certain type of hatching</u>, look at the map carefully and put a <u>big tick</u> on each part with that hatching, to make them all <u>stand out</u>. Look at this example for areas with more than 200 people per km^2:

4) When they ask you to <u>complete</u> part of one of the maps, first use the <u>key</u> to work out what type of shading you need. Use a <u>ruler</u> to draw in the lines, the same <u>angle</u> and <u>spacing</u> as in the key.

5) Choropleth maps are often used to show <u>population density</u> or <u>height of land</u>.

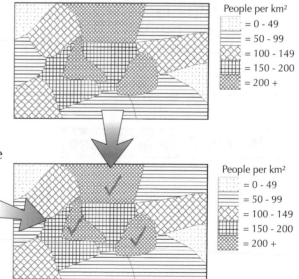

With topological maps you just need to be able to read them

Choropleths might not look it, but they're really quite friendly. The ticking trick is a good one for highlighting areas you need to discuss.

Types of Graphs and Charts

You'll come across <u>isolines</u> on maps... so you need to know what they are.

Isolines link up places with **Something** *in* **Common**

1) <u>Isolines</u> are lines on a map <u>linking</u> up all the places where something's the <u>same</u>.

2) <u>Contour lines</u> are isolines linking up places at the same <u>altitude</u>.

3) Isolines on a <u>weather map</u> link together all the places where the <u>atmospheric pressure</u> is the same (there's more about weather maps on p.43). These are known as <u>isobars</u>.

4) Isolines are flexible little fellows. They can be used to link up places where, say, <u>average temperature</u>, <u>wind speed</u>, <u>rainfall</u>, or <u>pollution levels</u> are the same.

Isolines can also be called isopleths, if you like.

1) How to Read an Isoline Map

EXAMPLE

Q: *Find the average annual rainfall in a) Port Portia, and b) Mt. Mapel.*

1) Find <u>Port Portia</u> on the map.

2) It's not on a line so look at the numbers on the lines <u>either side</u>. They're 200 and 400. Port Portia's about halfway between so the answer's <u>300 mm per year</u>.

3) The question about Mt. Mapel is much easier. It's bang on the line so the answer's <u>1000 mm per year</u>.

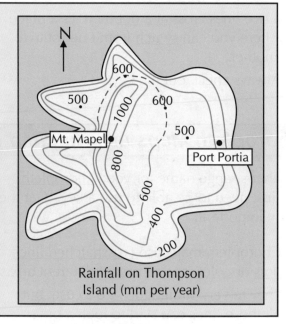

Rainfall on Thompson Island (mm per year)

2) How to Draw an Isoline

EXAMPLE

Q: *Complete on the map the line showing an average rainfall of 600 mm per year.*

1) Drawing an isoline's like doing a dot-to-dot where you join up all the dots with the <u>same numbers</u>.

2) Find all the dots marked 600, and the <u>half-finished line</u> with 600 on it.

3) Draw a neat <u>curvy</u> line joining up the <u>600s</u> and the two ends of the line.

4) Don't <u>cross</u> any other lines or <u>go past</u> the 500s. The correct answer is shown above as a <u>red dashed line</u>.

Isolines — a bit tougher, so get your head down

Not easy this, especially when you're looking something up that's not on a line.
If you have to <u>draw a line</u>, check the info on the map <u>before</u> you start drawing.

Questions

Nearly there... just three more pages to go. This is the last time, so have a go at the warm-up questions first to get your brain cells working, then have a go at the practice ones below.

Warm-up Questions

1) What are the main rules to use when describing a geographical photograph?

2) How do you read a bar chart?

3) How do you fill in a line graph?

4) What type of data do pie charts show?

5) What are the four things to look for when describing what graphs show?

Practice Questions

Here's six questions to make sure you've taken everything in this section in.

1) The bar graph shows the environmental quality for two different housing areas in a town. Look carefully at the graph and key.

Environmental Quality in Two Residential Areas in a Town

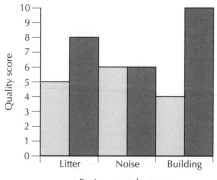

Key

Litter: 1 = lots of litter, 10 = no litter

Noise: 1 = lots of noise, 10 = little noise

Buildings: 1 = poor quality buildings
(e.g.; peeling paint, broken windows),
10 = good quality buildings

 = inner city

= suburbs

a) What is the total environmental quality score (the litter, noise and building scores added together) for the inner city area?

b) Draw a bar graph for a nearby village which has the following environmental scores: litter = 8, noise = 8, housing = 10.

c) Which residential area is the village most similar to?

2) a) Draw a <u>line graph</u> showing the changes in the birth rate in the UK using the following data:

Birth rate data for the UK 1760 - 1960

Year	1760	1780	1800	1820	1840	1860	1880	1900	1920	1940	1960
Birth rate per thousand	36	37	37	36	32	35	35	29	20	15	14

b) Describe the pattern on the graph.

Questions

Keep going... just four more practice questions to go.

3) Look at the pie chart below.
It shows the percentage of land taken up by different land uses in Doncaster's CBD.

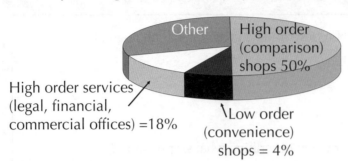

a) Which land use takes up the smallest area?

b) What is the total percentage of land covered by high order shops and high order services?

4) A survey was carried out to find out why people were in Doncaster's CBD.
The results were: shopping – 65%, work – 20%, leisure – 15%.
Make a pie chart which shows the results of the survey.

5) Look at the topological map. It shows the road pattern on McCallum.
Then answer the questions below.

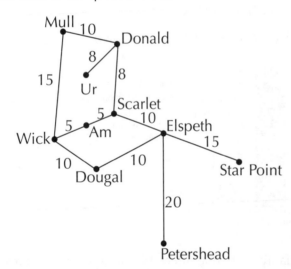

a) How far is it from Ur to Mull by the shortest possible route? (All distances are in km.)

b) Is there a direct route from Dougal to Scarlet?

c) You live at Wick and want to travel to Scarlet. The road from Am to Scarlet is shut. What is the shortest possible route between Wick and Scarlet?

6) The isoline map shows how many people were present in the town centre during a ten minute pedestrian count. Look at the isoline map and the street map of Doncaster's CBD.

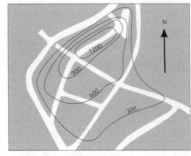 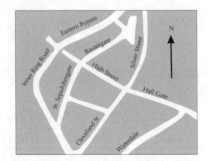

a) On which street were the most pedestrians counted?

b) How many pedestrians were there on Hall Gate?

Section Eleven — Summary Questions

With this section more than any other, you need to <u>practise practise practise</u>. Obviously you have to start by learning the <u>theory</u> of how to deal with maps and graphs. The best way to see whether you can do it is to try all these questions. When you've done them once, go back and learn any bits that you found tricky. Then do it all again. And again...

1) Write down the four-figure and six-figure grid references of all of the symbols marked on the OS® map that match the key.

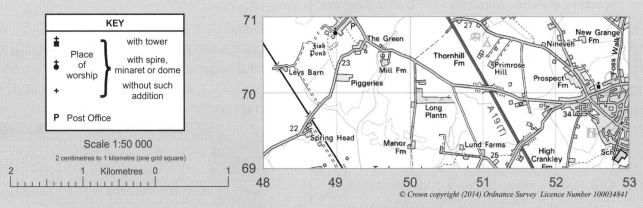

© Crown copyright (2014) Ordnance Survey Licence Number 100034841

KEY

Place of worship: with tower / with spire, minaret or dome / without such addition

P Post Office

Scale 1:50 000
2 centimetres to 1 kilometre (one grid square)

2) Using the above map, what is the distance along roads and paths in km, from the post office to
a) Manor Farm, b) Leys Barn, c) the nearest church?

3) Match each contour map with its corresponding shape.

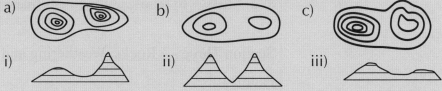

4) What kind of features would you use to work out how a photo matches a plan of the same area?

5)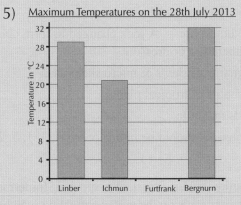

Maximum Temperatures on the 28th July 2013

a) What was the maximum temperature in Bergnurn?
b) Complete the graph to show that the maximum temperature in Furtfrank was 16°C.

6)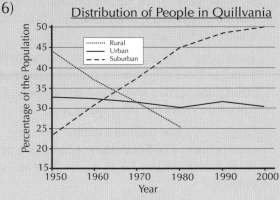

Distribution of People in Quillvania

a) What type of graph is this?
b) Complete the graph to show the rural population dropped to 22.5% in 1990 and 19.8% in 2000.
c) In what year was the percentage population in urban areas at its lowest?

Section Eleven — Geographical Enquiry and Skills

Section One — Locational Knowledge

Page 12

1) a) (A) Temperate grassland, (B) Savanna (tropical) grassland, (C) Coniferous forest, (D) Tropical rainforest.

b) A biome is an area with **distinctive** climate and vegetation. Biomes usually cover a **large** area, often spanning **multiple countries**. The United Kingdom is in an area of **deciduous forest**.

c) E.g. tundra. It can be found in northern Russia and Canada.

Page 13

2) a) Savanna grassland areas in Africa have wet and dry seasons. Temperatures are warm all year round but the wet season (20-30 °C) is warmer than the dry season (10-20 °C).

b) One of, e.g. grasses die down in the dry season / trees have long roots to reach the water table.

3)

Level of Development	Country	Life Expectancy	Literary Rate
Lower	Ethiopia	61 years	39%
Higher	Egypt	74 yeas	74%

4) Box 1

5) Statements b) and e) are true.

6) a) Turkey

b) Saudi Arabia

c) Iran

d) Oman

Section Two — Tectonic Activity

Page 24

1) The missing words, in the following order, are: long, millions, history, periods, larger.

2)

	Direction plates are moving	Type of boundary	Example
	Apart	Constructive	Mid-Atlantic Ridge (other answers possible)
	Together	Destructive	West coast of South America (other answers possible)
	Side by side	Conservative	San Andreas Fault (other answers possible)

3) a) False　b) True　c) False

Page 25

4) Focus — The point, usually below the surface of the earth, where an earthquake starts.

Epicentre — The point on the earth's surface above the focus, where the effect is strongest.

Richter scale — A system used to measure the size of earthquakes.

Seismometer — An instrument which detects vibrations.

5) a) Extinct — It will never erupt again.

b) Dormant — It's sleeping — it hasn't erupted for 2000 years.

c) Active — It has erupted recently and is likely to erupt again.

6)

	Shield	Dome	Composite
Sketch			
Made from	Runny, alkaline lava	Thick, acid lava	Lava and ash
Example	Mauna Loa, Hawaii	Mt. St. Helens	Mt. Etna

7) The missing words, in the following order, are: tectonic, collide, rock, mountains, mountain, high, steep.

8) a) True　b) False　c) True　d) True

Section Three — Rocks, Weathering and Soil

Page 34

1) a) Igneous — A rock made from molten material.

b) Sedimentary — A rock made from particles laid down in layers and compressed.

c) Metamorphic — A rock changed in form due to temperature or pressure.

2) a) Remains of shells & micro skeletons.

b) Remains of tropical plants.

c) Beds or Strata.

3) Sentences should be in this order: 4, 5, 1, 3, 2

Page 35

4) Granite — Very resistant to erosion; Impermeable, so water stays on the surface, creating marshes; Dartmoor has this type of rock; Soil is infertile and unsuitable for farming.

Limestone — Quarried for lime, cement and building blocks; Forms flat-topped moorlands with steep gorges; Also known as karst scenery; The Yorkshire Dales has this type of rock.

Chalk — Can be used as a natural reservoir; Forms escarpments; The South Downs has this type of rock; Soil is suitable for sheep farming and cereal crops.

5) a) dip slope   b) water trapped in the chalk
   c) scarp slope   d) spring line settlement

6) Texture can be sandy, clay, silt, etc. Structure can be of crumbly or blocky particles. Colour is black when there is a lot of organic matter. Acidity is measured in pH — usually 5 (acid) to 8 (alkaline).

Section Four — Weather and Climate

Page 47

1) The missing words, in the following order, are: climate change, constantly, 2.5 million, cold, an interglacial.

2) A — Arid / Deserts   B — Tropical
   C — Mediterranean   D — Temperate
   E — Tundra

3) a) Temperature usually decreases as you go higher up mountains.

   b) There is usually more rainfall on high ground than on lower ground.

   c) Coastal areas have a smaller temperature range than those further inland.

Page 48

4) Tropical — The table shows consistently high temperatures and rainfall levels, which is characteristic of a tropical climate.

5)

Weather	Measured using	Recorded in
Temperature	**thermometer**	degrees Celsius
Pressure	barometer	**millibars**
Precipitation	rain gauge	**millimetres**
Clouds	**observation**	coverage of sky

6) A — warm, wet onshore winds
   B — air rises and cools
   C — water vapour condenses
   D — drier air
   E — rain shadow area

7) a) True

   b) False — Heated air rises from the Earth's surface and causes rain.

   c) False — A cold front is where the cold air is pushing the warm air.

   d) True

   e) True

8) High pressure, because it brings dry conditions.

9) Lows have isobar readings which decrease in value towards the centre — highs are the opposite. Fronts are normally found only in lows.

Section Five — Hydrology, Coasts and Glaciation

Page 58

1) a) Rocks knock against each other and the bed, becoming smaller and more rounded.

   b) River material rubs against the bed and sides of the river banks.

   c) Chalk and limestone are dissolved in water.

   d) The force of the water wears away softer rocks like clay.

2) The river erodes less resistant rocks vertically in the upper stage. Falling water carves out a plunge pool at the base of the waterfall. The spray behind the waterfall helps to undercut and loosen material which falls into the plunge pool. The front of the waterfall collapses, so its position retreats upstream, creating a gorge. (Or similar explanation.)

3)

	a	b
speed	slow	fast
depth	shallow	deep
process	deposition	erosion
landform	beach (point bar)	cliff

4)

Advantages	Disadvantages
Controls flooding.	Spoils countryside.
Can be used to produce renewable energy.	Destroys settlements or farmland.
Can be used as a recreational resource.	Affects natural ecosystem.
	If the structure breaks there could be a disaster.

5) Soft engineering works with natural river processes to control water, whereas hard engineering uses man-made structures.

Page 68

1) **Constructive waves:** cause more deposition than erosion, operate in calmer weather, the swash is strong.

   Destructive waves: cause a lot of erosion, operate in storm conditions, the backwash is strong, can be several metres high.

2) a) Hydraulic action — Air and water are trapped and compressed in rock surface cracks when waves hit them. When the waves move away again, the air expands, weakening the rocks and breaking bits off.

   b) Wave pounding — The weight of waves acts like a battering ram.

   c) Attrition — Pieces of rock are ground down into smaller pieces until they become sand and are deposited as beaches.

d) Corrasion — Broken rock fragments in the waves are battered against the land, breaking off other pieces of rock.

e) Corrosion — Some types of rock react chemically with sea water and are dissolved.

3)

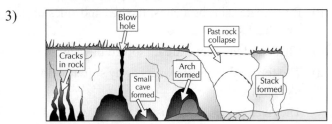

Page 69

4) **Hard engineering:** sea walls, gabions, armour blocks, revetments.

Soft engineering: managed retreat, shoreline vegetation, dune stabilisation, beach nourishment, set backs.

5) a) revetments   b) managed retreat   c) gabions

d) shoreline vegetation   e) dune stabilisation

6) a) 1 — corrie lake (tarn)   2 — corrie
   3 — arête   4 — waterfalls
   5 — flood plain   6 — truncated spur
   7 — hanging valley

b) A glacier changed this valley from a V shaped river valley to a U shaped glaciated valley by eroding it. The valley was eroded straighter and deeper. The ice cut through spurs making truncated spurs. Tributary valleys were left at a higher level, as hanging valleys, by the more powerful glacier in the main valley eroding down to a deeper level. (Or similar explanation.)

Section Six — Population and Urbanisation

Page 79

1) The following words should have been included in this order: uneven, wealthy, UK, Japan, poor, rapidly, India, Kenya, hostile, Antarctica. (Places are suggestions, accept other sensible answer.)

2) a) Overpopulation is when there are too many people in an area to be supported by the resources available.

b) Underpopulation is when there are too few people in an area to make the most of the resources available.

c) Optimum population is when there are adequate resources to support the number of people living in an area at a suitable standard of living.

Page 80

3) a) birth rate   b) death rate   c) migration

d) natural increase   e) natural decrease

4)

Description of Pyramid	Pyramid letter
An MEDC	D
An LEDC	A
A fast-growing capital city in an LEDC	B
An MEDC with a declining population	C

5) Push factors are things which make someone decide to leave their original home. E.g. unemployment, natural disasters, food shortage.

Pull factors are things which attract people to a new place. These are usually positive things. E.g. job prospects, the perception of a better standard of living and safety from a natural hazard.

6)

Term	Emigrant	Migrant	Immigrant
Definition	Someone moving out of a country, region or area.	Someone moving from one place to another.	**Someone moving into a country, region or area.**

Page 86

1) The correct words, in the following order, are: number, urban, more, richer, rural-urban.

2) a) Any two from:

There's often a shortage of services (e.g. education, water and power) in rural areas.

People from rural areas sometimes believe the standard of living is better in cities.

There are more jobs in urban areas.

If harvests fail in rural areas, farmers might have to move to feed their families.

b) In the past, new factories in urban areas created lots of jobs.

More recently, run-down inner city areas have been redeveloped, so they are more attractive places to live.

3) a) Relocation incentives are used to encourage people living in **large council houses** (who don't need them) to move out of urban areas. This **frees up houses** in urban areas for other people.

b) Brand new towns have been built to house the **overspill populations** from existing towns and cities where there was a **shortage of housing**.

c) **Urban renewal schemes** are government schemes to encourage investment in new housing, services and employment in derelict inner city areas.

Page 87

4) Improve access to the city centre, making public transport links and car parking better.
Improve public areas, e.g. parks, to make them more attractive.
Convert derelict warehouses into smart shops, restaurants and museums.
Pedestrianise areas to make them safer and nicer for shops.

5) Squatter settlements are settlements that are built illegally in and around cities in poorer countries, by people who can't afford proper housing. Life in a squatter settlement can be hard and dangerous as there's often no clean running water, sewers or electricity and no policing or medical services.

6)

Scheme	How it works
Self-help scheme	**These involve the government and local people working together to make improvements.**
Site & service scheme	**People pay a small amount of rent for a site, and they can borrow money to build or improve their house. The rent money is then used to provide basic services for the area.**
Local authority scheme	These are funded by the local government and are about improving the temporary accommodation built by residents.

7) Air pollution, any two from:
Acid rain.
Health problems (like headaches and bronchitis).
Destruction of the ozone layer.

Water pollution, any two from:
Kills fish and other aquatic animals.
Harmful chemicals build up in the food chain and can poison humans.
Spread of diseases like typhoid.

(Or other suitable answers.)

Section Seven — Development

Page 97

1) Words included should be: MEDCs, 80%.

2) Words should be in this order: North, developed, hemisphere, New Zealand, southern.

3)

Development Indicator	Meaning
Life expectancy	The average age that people can expect to live to.
Infant mortality rate	The number of babies who die before they are one year old per 1000 births.
Calorie intake	The average number of calories eaten per day.
Energy consumption	Number of British thermal units (Btu) used per person per year — an indication of level of industry.
Literacy rate	The percentage of adults who can read well enough to get by.

Page 98

4) It is difficult to compare countries using indicators because not all aspects of a country develop at the same rate. Also, there is not always up-to-date info for all countries, especially poorer ones that don't have the administration needed to collect it.

5) a) Locusts and famines
   b) Locusts
   c) Tropical storms (also volcanoes, earthquakes)
   d) Flooding (also volcanoes, earthquakes)

6) a) Raw materials have lower values than manufactured goods. As LEDCs have primary industries as the main source of income, there is little profit made.
   b) LEDCs selling their goods to MEDCs often get low prices for them.
   c) The price of raw materials fluctuates a lot on the international markets so LEDCs find it difficult to know how much income they can expect to receive from their primary industries.
   d) Demand for raw materials produced by LEDCs decreases.

7) Resources, more, less.

8) a) Bilateral aid is aid given directly from one government to another.
   b) Multilateral aid is aid given through agencies like the World Bank.
   c) Non-governmental aid is given through organisations like charities.

9) Development projects are schemes promoting development in LEDCs.

10) a) Small-scale projects are funded by governments or charities.
    b) Self-help projects aim to train people to do certain tasks so they can be self-sufficient in the future rather than relying on aid.

Section Eight — Economic Activity and the Use of Natural Resources

Page 113

1)

Type of industry	What it involves	Example 1	Example 2
Primary	Using raw materials	Fishing, mining, farming etc.	Fishing, mining, farming etc.
Secondary	Manufacturing a product	House building	Any manufacturing industry e.g. tyres, oil refining.
Tertiary	Providing a service	Advertising	Retailing, nursing, police, civil service etc.
Quaternary	Research and development	IT, genetic research etc.	Crop research

2) a) The New Zealand Forestry Company and Kutter & Company.

b) Baffin & Braithwaite bookshop.

c) Research best sort of trees to plant, grow trees, cut them down, make logs into paper, make paper into books, sell books.

d) False — they are a quaternary industry.

Page 114

3) a) Sustainable use of resources means using resources in a way that lets people living now have the things they need, but without reducing the ability of people in the future to meet their needs.

b) i) Resource　　ii) Substitution
iii) Pollution　　iv) Waste

4) Words should be in this order: natural resources, gas, coal (or coal, gas), electricity, power stations.

5) For: b, d, i　　Against: a, c, e, f, g, h

6) Any two of: banning wood from non-sustainable forestry; preventing illegal logging; encouraging businesses only to buy from sustainable forests (or any sensible answers).

Section Nine — Influencing the Environment

Page 125

1) a) A food chain is a series of links in an ecosystem.

b) Primary producer → herbivore → carnivore

c) E.g. humans can disrupt food chains by destroying habitats, through climate change or by over-exploiting one part of the chain (or any other sensible answers).

2) Words should be in this order: burning, carbon, respiration, plants, photosynthesis, use.

3)

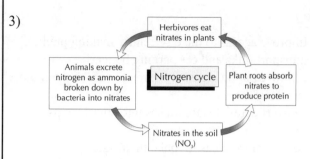

Page 126

4) sulphuric, water, chimneys, distance, wind

5) The following words should appear in this order:

a) Carbon dioxide and methane

b) Fossil fuels, carbon dioxide

c) Fossil fuels

d) Atmosphere

e) Temperature

6) a) Leaving stubble / planting new crops between rows reduces the area of vulnerable bare soil.

b) Stone lines following the contours of the land reduce run-off.

c) Strip farming means that crops are harvested at different times, which also minimises the amount of bare soil.

d) Shelter belts of trees act as windbreaks, and the roots hold the soil together and trap water.

e) Contour ploughing across hillsides means that run-off is slower.

f) Terracing is the building of flat areas into slopes, to help hold the water and soil.

Section Ten — A Study of Two Contrasting Regions

Page 138

1) a) Savanna grassland

b) Niger River

c) Mangroves

d) Benue River

e) Tropical rainforest

2) Nigeria's birth rate is **high** and the death rate is also **high**, but not as **high** as the birth rate. This means that the population is **growing**.

Page 139

3) A and C

4) There are over **6000** islands in Japan. It's a very **mountainous** country, and it lies on a **tectonic plate** boundary. Japan has a **temperate** climate like **the UK**.

5) B and C are true.
   Corrections: A Osaka is the **third** largest city in Japan OR **Tokyo** is the largest city in Japan.
   D The population of Osaka city is **declining**.

6) Any two of, e.g., Osaka and Lagos are both low-lying, both are coastal, both are at risk of flooding.

7) a) C
   b) A

Section Eleven — Geographical Enquiry and Skills

Page 145

1) Primary data is collected by **yourself**.
   Secondary data is collected by **others**.
   A traffic count is an example of **primary data**.

2) a) False.   b) True.   c) True.   d) False.

3) A questionnaire asks people a set of **questions** about a particular topic.

   A traffic count is when you count the number of **vehicles** per hour or per minute on a particular road.

   A **pedestrian** count is when you count the number of people who pass you per hour or per minute.

   Census data can tell you information about the **population.**

Page 151

1) a) 11 91   b) 07 88
   c) Downhill   d) Uphill

2) a) Gale Bank
   b) Brough Farm

Page 161

1) a) 15
   b)

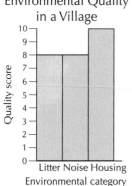

Environmental Quality in a Village

   c) Suburbs

2) a)

Line graph showing birth rates in the UK 1760 - 1960

   b) Birth rates have fallen from 36 per 1000 per year in 1760 to 14 per 1000 per year in 1960. At first the birth rate was steady and high. There was a sudden dip at about 1840. Birth rates climbed again but did not reach the same level as in 1760. Since 1880 there has been a steady decrease in birth rates. (Or a similar description.)

Page 162

3) a) Low order (convenience) shops   b) 68%

4)

Reasons for visiting Doncaster's CBD

Leisure 15%
Work 20%
Shopping 65%

5) a) 18 km   b) No   c) Via Dougal and Elspeth

6) a) Baxtergate   b) 300

Index

Index

Index